Mixer and Blender Cookery

HAMLYN

LONDON · NEW YORK · SYDNEY · TORONTO

Acknowledgements
Recipes created by Jill Spencer
Photography by John Lee
Cover picture by Iain Reid
Artwork by John Scott Martin
China kindly loaned by Royal Doulton Tableware Limited,
Denby Tableware Limited, David Mellor, Southern Electricity
Board (Hounslow), Josiah Wedgwood and Sons Limited

Published by
The Hamlyn Publishing Group Limited
London · New York · Sydney · Toronto
Astronaut House, Feltham, Middlesex, England

ISBN 0 600 36265 5

Printed in Spain by Printer industria gráfica sa
Sant Vicenç dels Horts   Barcelona   1978
Depósito Legal B. 746-1978

Contents

Introduction

An electric mixer and blender can be a great asset in the kitchen and this book has been compiled to show you how versatile these appliances can be and how you can get the maximum use from them.

There are basically three types of mixers available on the market – the large table models, hand-held models and the small mixers with a detachable stand and bowl. When choosing a mixer it is essential to bear the following points in mind. Firstly you must take into account the amount of beating, whisking, etc., you are going to want to use it for. If you have a growing family you will probably benefit from one of the large table models. Although these are more expensive, they are a good investment over the long term. An advantage of this type of mixer is that you can make, with ease, large batches of breads, cakes, biscuits and freeze some for future use. There are also optional attachments with this mixer which you can purchase at a later date.

The small hand-held mixers have been much improved over the years. However, they are not recommended for coping with very large quantities of ingredients. They are particularly useful for whisked mixtures such as sponges and meringues. Most appliances have three speeds.

The liquidiser (or blender) is a very versatile piece of equipment and probably is the most widely used of all kitchen gadgets. It takes the effort out of many mundane and time-consuming jobs such as making breadcrumbs, chopping, grinding and making purées.

Basically there are three types of liquidiser. One which fits the large table model mixer, free standing models and the smaller liquidiser which operates on the small hand mixer.

Make sure that you choose a liquidiser which can be cleaned easily. Some do not come apart and with these care has to be taken to clean under the blades. *Never put the electrical parts in water.* The quickest way to clean your liquidiser is to half fill the goblet with warm water and a drop of liquid detergent. Switch on for a few seconds, then detach, rinse and dry thoroughly.

The small liquidisers will only take small amounts of ingredients at a time. Generally the goblet should not be more than half full. Do not put very hot mixtures into the goblet. If the mixture creeps up the side of the goblet, stop and scrape it down to the blades. Always read the manufacturer's instructions as to the length of running times. It is always better to have several short bursts rather than one long one.

Be sure to cut solid foods into small pieces before dropping into the goblet and to do small quantities at a time. It is not advisable to chop raw meat, whisk egg whites or cream fat and sugar unless you have a very high powered liquidiser and the manufacturer recommends it.

Useful facts and figures

Notes on metrication

In this book quantities are given in metric, imperial and American measures. Exact conversion from imperial to metric measures does not usually give very convenient working quantities and so the metric measures have been rounded off into units of 25 grams. The table below shows the recommended equivalents.

Ounces	Approx. g to nearest whole figure	Recommended conversion to nearest unit of 25
1	28	25
2	57	50
3	85	75
4	113	100
5	142	150
6	170	175
7	198	200
8	227	225
9	255	250
10	283	275
11	312	300
12	340	350
13	368	375
14	397	400
15	425	425
16 (1 lb)	454	450
17	482	475
18	510	500
19	539	550
20	567	575

Note: When converting quantities over 10 oz first add the appropriate figures in the centre column, then adjust to the nearest unit of 25. As a general guide, 1 kg (1000 g) equals 2.2 lb or about 2 lb 3 oz. This method of conversion gives good results in nearly all cases but in certain pastry and cake recipes a more accurate conversion is necessary to produce a balanced recipe. On the other hand, quantities of such ingredients as vegetables, fruit, meat and fish which are not critical are rounded off to the nearest quarter of a kg as this is how they are likely to be purchased.

Liquid measures The millilitre has been used in this book and the following table gives a few examples:

Imperial	Approx. ml to nearest whole figure	Recommended ml
$\frac{1}{4}$ pint	142	150 ml
$\frac{1}{2}$ pint	283	300 ml
$\frac{3}{4}$ pint	425	450 ml
1 pint	567	600 ml
1$\frac{1}{2}$ pints	851	900 ml
1$\frac{3}{4}$ pints	992	1000 ml (1 litre)

Note: For quantities of 1$\frac{3}{4}$ pints and over we have used litres and fractions of a litre.

Spoon measures All spoon measures given in this book are level.

Can sizes At present, cans are marked with the exact (usually to the nearest whole number) metric equivalent of the imperial weight of the contents, so we have followed this practice when giving can sizes.

Oven temperatures

The table below gives recommended equivalents.

	°F	°C	Gas Mark
Very cool	225	110	$\frac{1}{4}$
	250	120	$\frac{1}{2}$
Cool	275	140	1
	300	150	2
Moderate	325	160	3
	350	180	4
Moderately hot	375	190	5
	400	200	6
Hot	425	220	7
	450	230	8
Very hot	475	240	9

Note: When making any of the recipes in this book, only follow one set of measures as they are not interchangeable.

Notes for American users

Although the recipes in this book give American measures, the lists below give some equivalents or substitutes for terms and commodities which may be unfamiliar to American readers.

Equipment and terms
BRITISH/AMERICAN

cake or loaf tin/cake or loaf pan
cling film/saran wrap
cocktail stick/toothpick
flan tin/pie pan
frying pan/skillet
greaseproof paper/waxed paper
grill/broil
kitchen paper/paper towels
liquidise/blend

mince/grind
packet/package
piping bag/pastry bag
polythene/plastic
roasting tin/roasting pan
sandwich tin/layer cake pan
stoned/pitted
top and tail/clean

Ingredients
BRITISH/AMERICAN

aubergine/eggplant
bacon rashers/bacon slices
bicarbonate of soda/baking soda
biscuit/cookie or cracker
black olives/ripe olives
black treacle/molasses
castor or granulated sugar/sugar
cocoa powder/unsweetened cocoa
cooking apples/baking apples
cordial/undiluted fruit drink
cornflour/cornstarch
courgette/zucchini
demerara sugar/brown sugar
digestive biscuits/graham crackers
double cream/heavy cream
essence/extract
gelatine/gelatin
gherkin/sweet dill pickle
gingernut biscuit/gingersnap
glacé cherry/candied cherry
ham/cured or smoked ham

hard-boiled eggs/hardcooked eggs
icing/frosting
icing sugar/confectioners' sugar
ketchup/catsup
mixed peel/candied peel
natural yogurt/unflavored yogurt
orange jelly/orange-flavored gelatin
plain chocolate/semi-sweet chocolate
plain flour/all-purpose flour
puff pastry/puff paste
self-raising flour/self rising flour
shortcrust pastry/basic pie dough
single cream/light cream
soda water/carbonated water
spring onion/scallion
stem ginger/preserved ginger
sultanas/seedless white raisins
tomato purée/tomato paste
topside of beef/top round of beef
unsalted butter/sweet butter

Note: The British and Australian pint is 20 fluid ounces as opposed to the American pint which is 16 fluid ounces.

Notes for Australian users

Ingredients in this book are given in cup, metric and imperial measures. In Australia the American 8-oz measuring cup is used in conjunction with the imperial pint of 20 fluid ounces. It is most important to remember that the Australian tablespoon differs from both the British and American tablespoons; the table below gives a comparison between the standard tablespoons used in the three countries. The British standard tablespoon holds 17.7 millilitres, the American 14.2 millilitres, and the Australian 20 millilitres. A teaspoon holds approximately 5 millilitres in all three countries.

British	American	Australian
1 teaspoon	1 teaspoon	1 teaspoon
1 tablespoon	1 tablespoon	1 tablespoon
2 tablespoons	3 tablespoons	2 tablespoons
3$\frac{1}{2}$ tablespoons	4 tablespoons	3 tablespoons
4 tablespoons	5 tablespoons	3$\frac{1}{2}$ tablespoons

Appetisers, soups and spreads

Most of the appetisers and spreads in this chapter have been devised to serve as starters or for informal entertaining with drinks. They are very quick to make and may be made in advance and stored in the refrigerator for 3–4 days, if you prefer.

Pâtés are an absolute must with a liquidiser and home-made soups are really worth making. No more messy sieving; all the nutrients remain in the soup making it full of goodness and tasty too.

Avocado pâté

METRIC/IMPERIAL/AMERICAN
3 avocado pears
225 g/8 oz/1 cup cream cheese
1 teaspoon lemon juice
1 tablespoon grated onion
pinch salt
freshly ground black pepper
100 g/4 oz/½ cup butter, melted

Halve, stone and peel the avocado pears. Slice one of the pears into six, toss in a little lemon juice and reserve for the garnish. Place the remaining avocados, the cheese, lemon juice, grated onion and seasoning in the liquidiser, and blend until smooth. Turn into individual dishes, pour a little melted butter over each and place a slice of avocado on top. Serve immediately with croûtons.

Serves 6

Smoked haddock pâté

METRIC/IMPERIAL/AMERICAN
450 g/1 lb/1 lb smoked haddock
175 g/6 oz/¾ cup cream cheese
75 g/3 oz/6 tablespoons butter, melted
grated rind of ½ lemon
1 tablespoon lemon juice
freshly ground black pepper
1 clove garlic, crushed
GARNISH:
wedges of lemon
1 bay leaf

Poach the haddock gently in a little water for about 10–15 minutes, until cooked. Drain, cool, remove the skin and flake the fish.

Place the flaked fish in the liquidiser with the cream cheese and melted butter. Blend until smooth. Add the remaining ingredients and continue to blend until the mixture is smooth. Turn the mixture into a serving dish, chill and garnish with wedges of lemon and a bay leaf.

Serves 6

Cod's roe pâté

METRIC/IMPERIAL/AMERICAN
1 slice white bread, crusts removed
2 (100-g/3½-oz/3½-oz) cans cod's roe
1 potato, boiled
1 clove garlic, crushed
few parsley sprigs
juice of ½ lemon
1 teaspoon grated onion
1 teaspoon oil
salt
freshly ground black pepper
4–6 lettuce leaves
GARNISH:
black olives
slices of lemon

Place the bread and cod's roe in the liquidiser and switch on to a high speed until well blended. Add the potato, garlic and parsley. Blend until smooth. Add the lemon juice, onion, oil and seasoning and continue to blend until smooth. Chill.

Place a lettuce leaf on individual plates, and spoon the pâté on top. Garnish with black olives and slices of lemon. Serve with fingers of toast.

Serves 4–6

Mackerel and soured cream pâté

METRIC/IMPERIAL/AMERICAN
225 g/8 oz/½ lb smoked mackerel
25 g/1 oz/2 tablespoons butter, melted
few drops of lemon juice
salt
freshly ground black pepper
few parsley sprigs
1 clove garlic, crushed
pinch nutmeg
2 tablespoons/2 tablespoons/3 tablespoons soured cream
grated rind of ½ lemon
few lettuce leaves
GARNISH:
slices of lemon
cress
radish roses

Remove the skin and the large bones from the mackerel. Cut into pieces and place in the liquidiser with the remaining ingredients, except the lettuce leaves. Blend until the pâté is smooth, then chill until firm.

Place the lettuce on four individual serving dishes, spoon the pâté on top of each and garnish with slices of lemon, cress and radish roses.

Serves 4

Cream cheese pâté with devilled biscuits

METRIC/IMPERIAL/AMERICAN
100 g/4 oz/½ cup cottage cheese
100 g/4 oz/½ cup cream cheese
1 clove garlic, crushed
1 tablespoon grated onion
salt
freshly ground black pepper
1 tablespoon chopped parsley
1–2 tablespoons/1–2 tablespoons/2–3 tablespoons milk or
    single cream
bay leaves to garnish
DEVILLED BISCUITS:
about 10 small water biscuits
50 g/2 oz/¼ cup butter
cayenne pepper

Place the cottage cheese with the remaining ingredients in the liquidiser and blend until smooth. Spoon into individual dishes and garnish with bay leaves.

To make the devilled biscuits, brush the water biscuits with a little melted butter and sprinkle with cayenne pepper. Place in a moderately hot oven (200°C, 400°F, Gas Mark 6) for 5 minutes. Serve with the cream cheese pâté.

Serves 4–6

Chicken and pork pâté

METRIC/IMPERIAL/AMERICAN
350 g/12 oz/¾ lb chicken livers
75 g/3 oz/6 tablespoons butter
2 cloves garlic
350 g/12 oz/¾ lb pork, chopped
175 g/6 oz/9 slices bacon, chopped
1 onion
25 g/1 oz/½ cup breadcrumbs
salt and pepper
1 egg
3 tablespoons/3 tablespoons/¼ cup brandy
½ teaspoon dried sage
225 g/8 oz/½ lb pork fat, cut into strips
bay leaf to garnish

Sauté the chicken livers in the butter with 1 clove of crushed
garlic for 2–3 minutes. Place in the liquidiser with any
remaining butter from the pan. Blend until smooth.

Mince the pork, bacon and onion. Stir in the breadcrumbs,
salt, black pepper, egg, brandy and sage.

Line an ovenproof dish with strips of pork fat, reserving
some for the top. Arrange layers of the pork mixture and
chicken livers in the dish finishing with the chicken livers.
Arrange strips of pork fat on the top in a lattice design. Place in
a baking tin filled with 2.5 cm (1 inch) water. Cook in a
moderate oven (180°C, 350°F, Gas Mark 4) for 1½–2 hours.
Allow to cool, then refrigerate.

Serves 6   *Illustrated on the cover*

French onion dip

METRIC/IMPERIAL/AMERICAN
225 g/8 oz/1 cup cream cheese
pinch curry powder to taste
1 (57-g/2-oz/2-oz) packet French onion soup
3–4 tablespoons/3–4 tablespoons/¼–⅓ cup boiling water
chopped parsley to garnish

Place the cream cheese and curry powder in the mixer bowl and
whisk together on a slow speed. Gradually mix in the remaining
ingredients. Turn into a serving dish and sprinkle with chopped
parsley.

Serve with prawns, stuffed olives and curried bread cubes to
dip.

Serves 4–6

Sardine cheese dip

METRIC/IMPERIAL/AMERICAN
2 (125-g/4¼-oz/4¼-oz) cans sardines
2 hard-boiled eggs
150 g/5 oz/generous 1 cup cream cheese
salt
freshly ground black pepper
few drops of lemon juice

Place all the ingredients in the liquidiser and blend until smooth. Chill.

Serve with sticks of raw celery, carrot or florets of cauliflower, spring onions, slices of apple and savoury biscuits.

Serves 6

Curd cheese creams

METRIC/IMPERIAL/AMERICAN
1 (290-g/10½-oz/10½-oz) can condensed consommé soup
15 g/½ oz/2 envelopes gelatine
175 g/6 oz/¾ cup curd cheese
pinch curry powder
1 tablespoon chopped chives
GARNISH:
slices of lemon
parsley sprigs

Place half the can of soup and gelatine in a saucepan and dissolve over a gentle heat. Cool and place in the liquidiser with the cheese and curry powder. Blend until smooth. Stir in the chives and pour into four individual ramekin dishes. Allow to chill for a few hours in the refrigerator.

Gently heat the remaining soup until liquid enough to pour on top of the chilled mixture. Allow to chill. Garnish each ramekin dish with a slice of lemon and a sprig of parsley. Serve with melba toast.

Note: These are even better if left to set in the refrigerator overnight.

Serves 4

Cheese pears

METRIC/IMPERIAL/AMERICAN
2 ripe pears
lemon juice
100 g/4 oz/½ cup cream cheese
1–2 tablespoons/1–2 tablespoons/1–3 tablespoons cream
salt and pepper
shredded lettuce
slices of radish to garnish

Peel the pears and slice in half lengthwise.

Remove the cores with a teaspoon and rub a little lemon juice over surface of the pears to prevent them discolouring. Place the cream cheese and cream in the mixer with the seasoning and switch on to a slow speed for 1–2 minutes. Pipe the mixture into the centre of each pear. Place some shredded lettuce on individual serving dishes with a pear half on top. Garnish with slices of radish.

Serves 4

Curried shrimp cocktails

METRIC/IMPERIAL/AMERICAN
150 ml/¼ pint/⅔ cup mayonnaise (see page 56)
1 teaspoon curry powder
225 g/8 oz/1 cup peeled shrimps
2 sticks celery, chopped
2 tomatoes, peeled and chopped
few lettuce leaves, shredded

Make the mayonnaise (see page 56) and stir in the curry powder, shrimps, celery and chopped tomatoes.

Place the shredded lettuce in the bottom of four individual serving glasses or dishes. Just before serving spoon the shrimp mixture on top.

Serves 4

Anchovy eggs

METRIC/IMPERIAL/AMERICAN
4 eggs, hard-boiled
2 tablespoons/2 tablespoons/3 tablespoons mayonnaise
  (see page 56)
1 (50-g/1¾-oz/1¾-oz) can anchovy fillets, drained
freshly ground black pepper
1 tablespoon chopped parsley
4 lettuce leaves
watercress
mayonnaise (optional)
pieces of tomato to garnish

Shell the eggs and cut in half lengthways. Carefully remove the
egg yolks and reserve the egg white halves. Place the yolks in
the liquidiser with the mayonnaise and anchovy fillets,
reserving four to garnish. Blend the mixture until smooth.

Stir in the black pepper and parsley. Pipe or spoon the
mixture into the egg white halves.

Place a lettuce leaf and watercress on four individual serving
dishes and place two egg halves on top.

Garnish with the reserved anchovies, rolled around a small
piece of tomato and serve with extra mayonnaise if liked.

Serves 4

Farmhouse vegetable soup

METRIC/IMPERIAL/AMERICAN
50 g/2 oz/¼ cup butter
3 medium onions, sliced
4 sticks celery, sliced
450 g/1 lb/1 lb potatoes, peeled and sliced
600 ml/1 pint/2½ cups chicken stock
bouquet garni
strip of lemon rind
pinch curry powder
salt and pepper
300 ml/½ pint/1¼ cups milk
chopped parsley to garnish

Melt the butter and sauté the vegetables for about 15–20
minutes, until soft. Pour over the stock and add the bouquet
garni, lemon rind, curry powder and seasoning. Bring to the
boil and simmer for 30 minutes.

Remove the bouquet garni and lemon rind. Allow to cool.

Pour into the liquidiser, a little at a time, and blend until
smooth. Return to the saucepan and stir in the milk; reheat
gently. Serve garnished with chopped parsley.

Serves 6

Chilled mulligatawny soup

METRIC/IMPERIAL/AMERICAN
75 g/3 oz/6 tablespoons butter
1 onion, finely chopped
1 carrot, finely chopped
75 g/3 oz/¾ cup flour
25 g/1 oz/¼ cup curry powder
scant 1.5 litres/2½ pints/6¼ cups beef stock
salt
freshly ground black pepper
florets of cauliflower to garnish

Melt the butter and sauté the vegetables until soft, but not browned.

Stir in the flour, curry powder and stock. Whisking all the time, bring to the boil. Cover and simmer for 30 minutes.

Allow to cool slightly, then pour into the liquidiser. Blend until smooth. Season to taste.

Chill and skim off any fat. Serve chilled garnished with florets of cauliflower.

Serves 6

Cream of lettuce soup

METRIC/IMPERIAL/AMERICAN
25 g/1 oz/2 tablespoons butter
2 lettuces, washed and shredded
1 onion, finely chopped
20 g/¾ oz/3 tablespoons flour
900 ml/1½ pints/3¾ cups milk
salt
freshly ground black pepper
2 egg yolks
4 tablespoons/4 tablespoons/⅓ cup cream

Melt the butter in a saucepan and add lettuce and onion. Cover and cook gently for 5 minutes. Add the flour and milk and, whisking all the time, bring to the boil. Reduce the heat and simmer for 15–20 minutes.

Allow to cool, then pour the soup into the liquidiser. Blend until smooth. Return to the saucepan and add the seasoning.

Mix the egg yolks and cream together and pour into the soup. Heat gently until thickened. Serve hot or cold with fried garlic croûtons.

Serves 4

Broccoli soup

METRIC/IMPERIAL/AMERICAN
450 ml/$\frac{3}{4}$ pint/2 cups chicken stock
1 (225-g/8-oz/8-oz) packet frozen broccoli
25 g/1 oz/2 tablespoons butter
2 teaspoons grated onion
25 g/1 oz/$\frac{1}{4}$ cup flour
600 ml/1 pint/2$\frac{1}{2}$ cups milk
150 ml/$\frac{1}{4}$ pint/$\frac{2}{3}$ cup single cream
salt
freshly ground black pepper

Bring the stock to the boil, add the broccoli and simmer until tender. Allow to cool slightly, then pour into the liquidiser. Blend until smooth.

Melt the butter, sauté the onion for 1 minute, remove from the heat and stir in the flour. Return to the heat and cook for 1 minute, still stirring. Gradually add the milk, stirring continuously and bring to the boil. Simmer for 2–3 minutes.

Stir in the blended broccoli and reheat. Add the cream and seasoning to taste.

Serves 4–6

Minted cucumber soup

METRIC/IMPERIAL/AMERICAN
1 cucumber
25 g/1 oz/2 tablespoons butter
15 g/$\frac{1}{2}$ oz/2 tablespoons flour
600 ml/1 pint/2$\frac{1}{2}$ cups chicken stock
salt
freshly ground black pepper
few mint sprigs
300 ml/$\frac{1}{2}$ pint/1$\frac{1}{4}$ cups milk
4 tablespoons/4 tablespoons/$\frac{1}{3}$ cup double cream

Peel the cucumber. Cut lengthways, remove the seeds and chop the flesh. Melt the butter and stir in the flour. Gradually add the stock and bring to the boil. Add the seasoning, mint and cucumber. Simmer for 10 minutes until tender. Allow to cool slightly then pour into the liquidiser. Blend until smooth.

Return to the saucepan, add the milk and reheat. Serve with the cream swirled on top.

Serve with puff pastry croûtons, made from left-over puff pastry cut into small squares and deep fried until golden brown.

Serves 4

Prawn spread

METRIC/IMPERIAL/AMERICAN
225 g/8 oz/1¼ cups peeled prawns or shrimps
1 tablespoon grated onion
50 g/2 oz/¼ cup butter
4 tablespoons/4 tablespoons/⅓ cup mayonnaise
1 tablespoon chopped parsley
few drops of lemon juice
100 g/4 oz/½ cup cream cheese
freshly ground black pepper
chopped parsley to coat

Place the prawns or shrimps in the liquidiser and blend until smooth. Add the remaining ingredients and continue blending until smooth. Turn into a mixing bowl and chill thoroughly, then form into a sausage shape. Coat in the chopped parsley and chill. Slice and serve with small savoury biscuits.

Serves 4–6

Guacamole

METRIC/IMPERIAL/AMERICAN
3 ripe avocado pears
1 small onion, finely chopped
1 tablespoon lemon juice
pinch chilli powder
salt
freshly ground black pepper
2 tomatoes, peeled and deseeded
chopped parsley to garnish

Halve, stone and peel the avocado pears. Place in the liquidiser with the onion, lemon juice and chilli powder and blend until smooth. Season to taste.

Roughly chop the peeled tomatoes and stir into the avocado mixture. Place in a serving dish and garnish with the chopped parsley.

Serve with stuffed olives, savoury biscuits and sticks of raw celery. This mixture may also be served as a spread on small savoury biscuits.

Serves 4

Main dishes

The mixer and liquidiser can be used to help speed up the preparation of many main course dishes.

Several recipes necessitate the use of breadcrumbs whether for coatings or for stuffings. These can be made in a matter of seconds in the liquidiser. Pastry can be made very successfully in the mixer, eliminating all the messy rubbing-in.

Batters are excellent made in the liquidiser and a mixer takes the hard work out of preparing soufflés.

Crispy fried fish balls

METRIC/IMPERIAL/AMERICAN
50 g/2 oz/$\frac{1}{4}$ cup butter
50 g/2 oz/$\frac{1}{2}$ cup flour
150 ml/$\frac{1}{4}$ pint/$\frac{2}{3}$ cup milk
350 g/12 oz/$\frac{3}{4}$ lb smoked haddock, cooked
grated rind of $\frac{1}{2}$ lemon
salt and pepper
1 tablespoon chopped parsley
2 hard-boiled eggs, chopped
COATING:
beaten egg
fresh white breadcrumbs

oil for deep frying

Place the butter, flour and milk in the liquidiser and switch on to maximum speed for 30 seconds. Pour into a saucepan and, whisking all the time, bring to the boil. Simmer gently for 1 minute. Stir in the remaining ingredients and then spread over a plate and mark into 12 portions. Chill until firm enough to handle.

Roll into balls, using a little flour if necessary. Dip in the beaten egg and then toss in the breadcrumbs.

Heat the oil to 180°C/360°F and fry the fish balls until golden. Drain well on absorbent paper. Serve with tomato sauce (see page 54).
Note: These fish balls may be cooked fondue style at the table.

Serves 4

Curried haddock croquettes

METRIC/IMPERIAL/AMERICAN
225 g/8 oz/½ lb haddock fillets, poached
25 g/1 oz/2 tablespoons butter
1 shallot, finely chopped
1 teaspoon curry powder
25 g/1 oz/¼ cup plain flour
150 ml/¼ pint/⅔ cup milk
salt and pepper
COATING:
beaten egg
fresh white breadcrumbs

oil for deep frying

Remove the skin and bones from the poached haddock and flake the flesh. Melt the butter and sauté the shallot for 2–3 minutes. Stir in the curry powder and cook for a further minute. Gradually stir in the flour and milk and, stirring all the time, bring to the boil and cook for 1 minute. Add the flaked haddock and seasoning. Spread mixture on to a plate and chill in the refrigerator until cold.

Taking spoonfuls of the mixture, shape into croquettes using a little flour if necessary. Toss in beaten egg and then coat in breadcrumbs made in the liquidiser. Heat the oil to 180°C/360°F and fry croquettes until golden brown. Drain on absorbent paper.

Serves 4

Prawn pancakes

METRIC/IMPERIAL/AMERICAN
PANCAKES:
300 ml/½ pint/1¼ cups milk
3 eggs
100 g/4 oz/1 cup plain flour
pinch salt
FILLING:
25 g/1 oz/2 tablespoons butter
25 g/1 oz/¼ cup plain flour
300 ml/½ pint/1¼ cups milk
pinch ground mace
1 teaspoon tomato purée
1 tablespoon chopped parsley
225 g/8 oz/1¼ cups peeled prawns
cress to garnish

Place the pancake ingredients in the liquidiser and blend until smooth. Lightly brush an omelette pan with a little oil and heat. Pour a little of the batter into the pan, enough to cover the base. Cook on each side. Continue until all the batter is used. Keep hot with a sheet of greaseproof between each pancake.

Place the butter, flour, milk, mace, tomato purée and parsley in the liquidiser and switch on to maximum speed for 30 seconds. Pour into a saucepan and whisking all the time over a moderate heat, bring to the boil. Simmer for 1 minute, stirring. Stir in the prawns. Form the pancakes into triangles and fill the top pocket with the prawn mixture. Garnish.

Serves 4

Prawn and apple quiche

METRIC/IMPERIAL/AMERICAN
MIXER PASTRY:
150 g/5 oz/generous ½ cup margarine
225 g/8 oz/2 cups plain flour
FILLING:
1 medium onion, chopped
3 rashers streaky bacon, chopped
100 g/4 oz/¾ cup peeled prawns
50 g/2 oz/½ cup Cheddar cheese, grated
1 medium eating apple, peeled, cored and chopped
2 eggs
150 ml/¼ pint/⅔ cup single cream
seasoning and chopped chives
parsley, prawns and slices of apple to garnish

Place the margarine, 2–3 tablespoons water and one-third of the flour in the mixer bowl. Using a slow speed combine the ingredients together until just mixed. Add the remaining flour and mix again until a dough is formed. Knead lightly on a floured board and roll out and line a 20-cm/8-inch flan dish. Bake blind in a moderately hot oven (200°C, 400°F, Gas Mark 6) for 15–20 minutes. Sauté the onion and bacon in oil until crisp, drain. Sprinkle over the base of the flan case with the prawns, cheese and apple. Place the eggs and cream in the mixer bowl with the seasoning and chives and whisk until frothy. Pour into flan case. Reduce the oven temperature to 190°C, 375°F, Gas Mark 5 and bake for 30–40 minutes. Garnish.

Serves 4–6

Crab mousse

METRIC/IMPERIAL/AMERICAN
300 ml/½ pint/1¼ cups white sauce (see page 53)
2 tablespoons/2 tablespoons/3 tablespoons tomato purée
1 teaspoon anchovy essence
few drops of lemon juice
1 (212-g/7½-oz/7½-oz) can crabmeat, boned and flaked
½ cucumber, skinned and diced
15 g/½ oz/2 envelopes gelatine
4 tablespoons/4 tablespoons/⅓ cup water
3 eggs, separated
150 ml/¼ pint/⅔ cup double cream
GARNISH:
slices of cucumber
watercress sprigs

Make the sauce and beat in the tomato purée, anchovy essence and lemon juice. Stir in the crabmeat and cucumber.

Dissolve the gelatine in the water in a small bowl placed over a saucepan of hot water. Allow to cool slightly. Stir the gelatine into the crab mixture with the egg yolks.

Place the egg whites in the mixer bowl and whisk until fairly stiff. Whisk the cream until lightly whipped. When the crab mixture is on the point of setting, carefully fold in the egg whites and cream. Pour into a ring mould and chill in the refrigerator until set. Turn out and garnish with slices of cucumber and watercress sprigs.

Serves 4–6

Stuffed plaice mimosa

METRIC/IMPERIAL/AMERICAN
4 slices white bread, crusts removed
2 hard-boiled eggs
few parsley sprigs
50 g/2 oz/$\frac{1}{2}$ cup cheese, grated
50 g/2 oz/$\frac{1}{4}$ cup butter, melted
salt
freshly ground black pepper
2 plaice, filleted and skinned
broccoli spears to garnish

Place the bread in the liquidiser and make into breadcrumbs. Roughly chop the eggs and add to the breadcrumbs with the parsley. Blend for a few seconds only. Turn into a bowl and stir in the cheese, melted butter and seasoning. Mix well together.

Spread the filling over the skinned side of each fillet and roll up, starting at the tail end. Secure with a wooden cocktail stick and place in a greased ovenproof dish. Cook in a moderate oven (180°C, 350°F, Gas Mark 4) for 15–20 minutes. Remove the cocktail sticks, garnish with broccoli spears and serve with parsley sauce (see page 53).

Serves 4

Puff top fish pie

METRIC/IMPERIAL/AMERICAN
2 sticks celery, chopped
1 onion, chopped
75 g/3 oz/6 tablespoons butter
675 g/1$\frac{1}{2}$ lb/1$\frac{1}{2}$ lb smoked cod or haddock, cubed
450 ml/$\frac{3}{4}$ pint/2 cups milk
25 g/1 oz/$\frac{1}{4}$ cup flour
salt and pepper
1 egg yolk
1 tablespoon cream
3 tablespoons/3 tablespoons/$\frac{1}{4}$ cup chopped parsley
75 g/3 oz/$\frac{3}{4}$ cup cheese, grated
1 (212-g/7$\frac{1}{2}$-oz/7$\frac{1}{2}$-oz) packet frozen puff pastry
twist of lemon and watercress sprigs to garnish

Sauté the vegetables in 50 g/2 oz/$\frac{1}{4}$ cup of the butter until softened. Stir in the fish and simmer for 5 minutes. Add the milk, bring to the boil and simmer for 10 minutes. Drain and reserve liquor. Place the remaining butter, the flour and strained fish liquor in the liquidiser. Blend until smooth then pour into a saucepan. Bring to the boil, whisking all the time. Stir in the vegetables, fish, seasoning, egg yolk, cream, parsley and cheese. Pour into an ovenproof dish; cool. Roll out the pastry and cut out 5-cm/2-inch circles. Overlap them around the edge of the dish. Brush with milk and bake in a hot oven (230°C, 450°F, Gas Mark 8) for 15–25 minutes.

Serves 4–6

Baked stuffed mackerel

METRIC/IMPERIAL/AMERICAN
4 mackerel, boned and with heads removed
STUFFING:
50 g/2 oz/¼ cup butter
1 onion, chopped
3 sticks celery, chopped
3 slices white bread, crusts removed
few parsley sprigs
grated rind of ½ lemon
pinch mixed herbs
1 egg
watercress sprigs and twists of lemon to garnish

Melt the butter and sauté the onion and celery until soft. Place the bread in the liquidiser and blend into fine breadcrumbs. Add the parsley, seasoning, lemon rind, herbs, egg and sautéed vegetables and blend together. Spread the stuffing on to the flesh side of each mackerel and roll up, starting at the head end. Place the stuffed fish in an ovenproof dish. Pour a little water in the dish just to cover the base. Cook in a moderately hot oven (190°C, 375°F, Gas Mark 5) for 20–25 minutes.

For a gooseberry sauce, place 450 g/1 lb/4 cups prepared gooseberries in a pan with 2–3 tablespoons water and 15 g/½ oz/ 1 tablespoon butter. Simmer until cooked; cool and then liquidise until smooth. Return to the pan, add 25 g/1 oz/ 2 tablespoons castor sugar and reheat. Serve with the mackerel. Garnish.

Serves 4

Liver and bacon terrine

METRIC/IMPERIAL/AMERICAN
225 g/8 oz/½ lb bacon rashers, derinded
1 slice white bread, crusts removed
1 small onion, quartered
few parsley sprigs
100 g/4 oz/¼ lb lamb's liver, chopped
100 g/4 oz/½ cup sausagemeat
100 g/4 oz/¼ lb lean pork, chopped
salt and pepper
pinch nutmeg
beaten egg to bind
225 g/8 oz/½ lb cooked chicken, sliced
bay leaves to garnish

Line an 18-cm/7-inch round cake tin with foil. Stretch the bacon rashers with a knife and place on the foil.

Place the bread, onion and parsley in the liquidiser and blend until the mixture forms fine breadcrumbs. Turn into a bowl and add the liver, sausagemeat, pork, seasoning and sufficient egg to make a soft consistency.

Starting with a layer of sliced chicken, alternate with layers of the meat mixture to fill the tin. Cover with foil and place in a baking tin half filled with water. Bake in a moderate oven (160°C, 325°F, Gas Mark 3) for 2–2½ hours. Cover with a plate with weights on top and when cool, place in the refrigerator overnight. Turn out of the tin and remove foil. Garnish with bay leaves and serve with a salad.

Serves 6–8

Savoury meat loaf

METRIC/IMPERIAL/AMERICAN
25 g/1 oz/2 tablespoons butter or margarine
175 g/6 oz/¾ cup onions, diced
75 g/3 oz/¾ cup mushrooms, chopped
25 g/1 oz/¼ cup plain flour
175 ml/6 fl oz/¾ cup milk
2 eggs
1 teaspoon Worcestershire sauce
salt and pepper
1 teaspoon mixed herbs
3 tablespoons/3 tablespoons/¼ cup tomato purée
1 tablespoon chopped parsley
450 g/1 lb/2 cups minced beef
175 g/6 oz/¾ cup minced pork
75 g/3 oz/1½ cups fresh white breadcrumbs
slices of tomato and cucumber, radish roses, lettuce, cress
   to garnish

Melt the butter or margarine and sauté the onions until soft but
not browned. Stir in the mushrooms and flour and cook for 1
minute. Add the milk gradually, stirring all the time and bring
to the boil. Allow to cool slightly.

Add the remaining ingredients to the cooked mixture and
mix well together. Place in a 1-kg/2-lb greased loaf tin and cook
in a moderate oven (180°C, 350°F, Gas Mark 4) for 1–1¼ hours.
Allow to cool slightly in the tin before turning out. When cold
wrap in foil and chill. Garnish before serving.

Serves 4–6

Beef olives

METRIC/IMPERIAL/AMERICAN
1 onion, chopped roughly
1 slice bread, crusts removed
few parsley sprigs
1 teaspoon mixed herbs
175 g/6 oz/1 cup pork, minced
1 apple, peeled, cored and finely chopped
1 egg, beaten
8 thin slices beef topside
2 tablespoons/2 tablespoons/3 tablespoons oil
2 onions, chopped
4 tomatoes, peeled and chopped
300 ml/½ pint/1¼ cups red wine or stock
slices of tomato and cress to garnish

Place the onion, bread and parsley in the liquidiser and blend for
30 seconds. Add the herbs, pork, apple, seasoning and beaten
egg. Divide the stuffing between the slices of meat, and spread
evenly. Roll up and secure with string. Heat the oil and sauté
the beef olives until brown. Remove, add the vegetables and
sauté for 5 minutes. Place vegetables and beef olives in a
casserole. Pour over wine, cover and cook in a moderate oven
(180°C, 350°F, Gas Mark 4) for 1–1½ hours.

Remove olives and keep hot. Pour the sauce and vegetables
into the liquidiser and blend until smooth. Reheat and pour
over the beef olives. Pipe a border of potato around edge of the
beef olives and serve garnished.

Serves 4–8

Beef and walnut cobbler

METRIC/IMPERIAL/AMERICAN
675 g/1½ lb/1½ lb chuck steak, cubed
25 g/1 oz/¼ cup seasoned flour
100 g/4 oz/½ cup margarine
2 onions, sliced
1 clove garlic, crushed
1 green pepper, sliced
450 ml/¾ pint/2 cups beef stock
1½ tablespoons tomato purée
225 g/8 oz/2 cups plain flour
½ teaspoon bicarbonate of soda
1 teaspoon cream of tartar
1 egg, beaten
5 tablespoons/5 tablespoons/6 tablespoons milk
25 g/1 oz/¼ cup walnuts, chopped

Toss the meat in seasoned flour. Melt half the margarine and
sauté the vegetables for 5 minutes. Remove. Brown the meat,
then replace the vegetables; add seasoning, stock and the
tomato purée. Cover and cook in a moderately hot oven (190°C,
375°F, Gas Mark 5) for 1½ hours. Place the remaining
margarine, flour, pinch salt, bicarbonate, cream of tartar, egg
and milk in the mixer bowl and switch on to a slow speed to
form a soft dough. Knead lightly and roll out and cut into 5-
cm/2-inch circles. Place overlapping on top of the meat, glaze
and sprinkle with the walnuts. Return to a hot oven (220°C,
425°F, Gas Mark 7) for 20–25 minutes. Garnish with parsley.

Serves 4–6

Guard of honour with apricot stuffing

METRIC/IMPERIAL/AMERICAN
2 joints best end neck of lamb, chined
4 slices white bread, crusts removed
few sprigs parsley and mint
40 g/1½ oz/3 tablespoons margarine
1 small onion, chopped
75 g/3 oz/½ cup dried apricots, chopped
salt and pepper
beaten egg to bind
broccoli spears to garnish

Choose joints of lamb with six or seven chops on each. Trim the
bones to within 2.5 cm/1 inch of the top. Place the joints
together allowing the bones to cross alternately with the bases
together. Secure with string.

Place the bread in the liquidiser with the parsley and mint.
Switch on to a medium speed for 6–8 seconds. Turn into a
bowl. Melt the margarine and sauté the onion. Stir into the
breadcrumb mixture with the remaining ingredients, adding
egg to bind.

Fill the cavity between the two joints of meat with the
stuffing. Cover the end of each bone with foil to prevent
burning. Place the meat in a roasting tin and roast in a
moderately hot oven (190°C, 375°F, Gas Mark 5) for 1¼–1½
hours. Remove the foil and replace with cutlet frills.

Serves 6

Stuffed lamb chops

METRIC/IMPERIAL/AMERICAN
4 loin lamb chops
STUFFING:
2 slices white bread, crusts removed
few mint sprigs
few rosemary sprigs
½ small onion, roughly chopped
grated rind of ½ lemon
beaten egg to bind
GARNISH:
watercress sprigs
quarters of tomato

Slit the chops horizontally through to the bone, to form a pocket.

Place the bread in the liquidiser with the remaining ingredients and switch on to a medium speed. Blend until a fairly moist stuffing is formed. Divide into four and fill the cavity in each of the chops. Wrap each one in foil. Cook in a moderately hot oven (190°C, 375°F, Gas Mark 5) for 20–25 minutes. Unwrap and garnish with watercress sprigs and quarters of tomato. Serve with sautéed mushrooms.

Serves 4

Minted lamb and apricot kebabs

METRIC/IMPERIAL/AMERICAN
MARINADE:
175 ml/6 fl oz/¾ cup oil
4 tablespoons/4 tablespoons/⅓ cup wine vinegar
1 clove garlic, crushed
few fresh mint leaves
salt and pepper
few parsley sprigs
KEBABS:
675 g/1½ lb/1½ lb lean leg of lamb, cubed
8 bay leaves
4 courgettes, sliced thickly
12 dried apricots, soaked overnight in cold water and drained

Place all the marinade ingredients in the liquidiser and blend until smooth. Place the lamb in a shallow dish, pour over the marinade and set aside in the refrigerator for 1–2 hours.

Thread the lamb and the remaining ingredients on to four long skewers. Brush with the marinade and cook under a hot grill, turning and basting the kebabs frequently.

Serve with barbecue sauce (see page 54).

Serves 4

Apricot and garlic lamb

METRIC/IMPERIAL/AMERICAN
50 g/2 oz/¼ cup butter
1 large clove garlic, crushed
3 slices white bread, crusts removed
few parsley sprigs
few rosemary sprigs
1 onion, roughly chopped
50 g/2 oz/⅓ cup dried apricots, chopped
1 egg, beaten
salt and pepper
2-kg/4½-lb/4½-lb leg lamb, boned
50 g/2 oz/¼ cup white fat
watercress sprigs to garnish

Mix the butter and garlic and form into a roll. Wrap in foil and chill until hard. Place the bread, parsley, rosemary and onion in the liquidiser and blend for 30 seconds. Turn into a basin and stir in the egg and seasoning.

Place the garlic butter in the cavity in the lamb, and surround with the stuffing. Secure the lamb with skewers. Calculate the cooking time of the stuffed lamb allowing 20 minutes per 0.5 kg/1 lb plus 20 minutes over.

Melt the white fat in a roasting tin, place the meat in the tin and baste well. Cook in a hot oven (220°C, 425°F, Gas Mark 7) for 20 minutes. Reduce heat to moderately hot (190°C, 375°F, Gas Mark 5) to finish cooking. Garnish.

Serves 6

Crispy pork chops in a basket

METRIC/IMPERIAL/AMERICAN
4 pork chops
3 slices bread, crusts removed
few parsley sprigs
small bunch fresh tarragon leaves
salt and pepper
1 egg, beaten
75 g/3 oz/6 tablespoons butter
2 tablespoons/2 tablespoons/3 tablespoons oil
watercress sprigs to garnish

Trim the chops, removing the fat from the end of the bone.

Place the bread, parsley and tarragon in the liquidiser and blend for 30 seconds. Season lightly. Coat each chop in beaten egg, then dip into the breadcrumb mixture.

Heat the butter and oil and gently fry the chops until crisp and golden, about 15–20 minutes depending on the thickness of the chops. Serve on a napkin placed in a basket and garnish with watercress sprigs. Accompany with barbecue sauce (see page 54), if liked.

Serves 4

Chicken and herb soufflé

METRIC/IMPERIAL/AMERICAN
4 eggs, separated
salt and pepper
2 tablespoons/2 tablespoons/3 tablespoons lemon juice
1 (298-g/10½-oz/10½-oz) can condensed asparagus soup
225 g/8 oz/2 cups cucumber, chopped
225 g/8 oz/1 cup cooked chicken, chopped
½ teaspoon tarragon
25 g/1 oz/4 envelopes gelatine
chopped parsley to garnish

Place the egg yolks, seasoning and lemon juice in a bowl over a saucepan of hot water. Whisk until thick and creamy. Stir in the soup, cucumber, chicken and tarragon.

Dissolve the gelatine in 4 tablespoons/4 tablespoons/⅓ cup water in a small bowl over a saucepan of hot water; cool slightly, then fold into the chicken mixture.

Whisk the egg whites until fairly stiff, then fold into the mixture. Pour into a 15-cm/6-inch soufflé dish with a band of double greaseproof paper tied around, standing 7.5 cm/3 inches above the rim of the dish and a 450-g/1-lb jam jar placed in the centre. Chill until set.

Carefully remove the greaseproof paper, easing it away from the soufflé with a palette knife. To remove the jar, give a sharp twist to loosen edges and carefully lift out. Fill the centre with chopped apple and olives; press chopped parsley into the edges.

Serves 4–6

Curried chicken mayonnaise

METRIC/IMPERIAL/AMERICAN
300 ml/½ pint/1¼ cups mayonnaise (see page 56)
curry powder to taste
single cream or top of the milk
4 cooked chicken portions
GARNISH:
shredded lettuce
pieces of cucumber skin cut into leaves and stalks
orange rind cut into flowers
slices of cucumber

Make the mayonnaise and stir in the curry powder to taste. Thin down with cream or top of the milk until it forms a coating consistency.

Skin the chicken and remove any fat or gristle. Place the chicken portions on a wire tray and spoon the mayonnaise over evenly.

Serve on a bed of shredded lettuce and garnish each chicken portion with leaves and stalks of cucumber skin and orange rind flowers. Garnish the dish with slices of cucumber and serve with garlic bread.

Serves 4

Chicken gougère

METRIC/IMPERIAL/AMERICAN
150 ml/¼ pint/⅔ cup water
50 g/2 oz/¼ cup butter
65 g/2½ oz/generous ½ cup plain flour
2 eggs, beaten
1 onion, chopped
15 g/½ oz/2 tablespoons butter
25 g/1 oz/¼ cup flour
300 ml/½ pint/1¼ cups milk
450 g/1 lb/2 cups cooked chicken, chopped
2 hard-boiled eggs, chopped
1½ tablespoons chopped parsley
grated rind of ½ lemon
1 tablespoon each breadcrumbs and grated cheese
25 g/1 oz/¼ cup flaked almonds

Heat the water and butter. Bring to the boil, remove and beat in the flour and seasoning until the mixture leaves the sides of the pan. Cool then place in the mixer bowl. Add eggs with the mixer on slow speed. Place in a piping bag with a 1-cm/½-inch plain nozzle and pipe two rows around edges of four 13-cm/5-inch ovenproof dishes. Cook in a hot oven (220°C, 425°F, Gas Mark 7) for 20 minutes. Sauté the onion in the butter until soft. Stir in the flour and cook for 1 minute. Gradually stir in the milk and bring to the boil. Add the chicken, eggs, parsley and lemon rind. Spoon into the dishes. Mix the breadcrumbs, cheese and almonds and sprinkle over. Bake for 5–10 minutes.

Serves 4

Cheese and herb soufflé

METRIC/IMPERIAL/AMERICAN
50 g/2 oz/¼ cup butter or margarine
50 g/2 oz/½ cup flour
300 ml/½ pint/1¼ cups milk
salt and pepper
1 tablespoon chopped parsley
½ teaspoon basil
pinch dry mustard
3 eggs, separated
100 g/4 oz/1 cup Cheddar cheese, grated
parsley sprig to garnish

Place the butter or margarine, flour and milk in the liquidiser and switch on to maximum speed for 30 seconds. Pour into a saucepan and whisking all the time bring to the boil. Simmer gently for 1 minute, still stirring. Stir in the seasoning, parsley, basil and mustard. Allow to cool slightly.

Pour the sauce into the mixer bowl and whisk in the egg yolks. Fold in the grated cheese. Whisk the egg whites until stiff, then fold into the mixture. Pour into 4 greased individual ramekin dishes and cook in a moderately hot oven (190°C, 375°F, Gas Mark 5) for 20–25 minutes. Serve immediately garnished with parsley.

Serves 4

Fluffy omelettes

METRIC/IMPERIAL/AMERICAN
2 eggs, separated
2 tablespoons/2 tablespoons/3 tablespoons water
pinch mixed herbs
salt and pepper
15 g/½ oz/1 tablespoon butter
watercress sprigs to garnish

Place the egg yolks in the mixer bowl with the water, herbs and
seasoning. Whisk until creamy. Whisk the egg whites until stiff,
then fold into the egg yolk mixture. Melt the butter in an
omelette pan. Pour in the egg mixture and cook for 1–2
minutes. Place under a hot grill for a few seconds to allow the
top to set. Place the chosen filling on one half and fold in two.
Slide the omelette out of the pan on to a heated plate and serve
garnished with watercress sprigs.

Serves 1

Fillings
1 50 g/2 oz/½ cup grated Cheddar cheese – sprinkle on to the
omelette before placing it under the grill.
2 50 g/2 oz/¼ cup peeled prawns blended with a little cream.
3 1 tomato, peeled, sliced and sautéed with 1 chopped onion.
4 50 g/2 oz/¼ cup cooked smoked haddock mixed with 1 2
tablespoons chopped parsley.
5 2 kidneys sliced and sautéed in butter then mixed with a little
sherry and tomato purée.

Provençal onions

METRIC/IMPERIAL/AMERICAN
4 medium onions, peeled
4 slices white bread, crusts removed
1 clove garlic, crushed
salt
freshly ground black pepper
50 g/2 oz/½ cup cheese, grated
1 egg, beaten
25 g/1 oz/2 tablespoons butter
chopped parsley to garnish

Cook the onions in boiling salted water for 15–20 minutes,
taking care not to let them get too soft. Drain and allow to cool.
   Place the bread in the liquidiser and make into breadcrumbs.
Turn into a basin and add the garlic, seasonings and half of the
cheese. Using a pointed knife scoop out the centres of the
onions. Chop the centres finely and mix with the breadcrumb
mixture. Moisten with the beaten egg. Fill the onions with the
stuffing and place in a greased ovenproof dish. Place a knob of
butter on top of each onion and sprinkle with the remaining
cheese. Cook in a moderate oven (180°C, 350°F, Gas Mark 4)
for 20–30 minutes. Garnish with chopped parsley and serve
with tomato sauce (see page 54).

Serves 4

Hot and cold puddings

Puddings can be a real joy to make with the aid of a mixer or liquidiser. You can make soufflés and meringues at the flick of a switch.

Fruit purées and biscuit crumb crusts can be made in a matter of seconds. Nuts can be chopped finely or coarsely as required, and almonds can be made into ground almonds.

Pineapple fritters

METRIC/IMPERIAL/AMERICAN
FRITTER BATTER:
50 g/2 oz/$\frac{1}{2}$ cup plain flour
1 egg, separated
5 tablespoons/5 tablespoons/6 tablespoons milk
1 tablespoon water

oil for deep frying
1 (439-g/15$\frac{1}{2}$-oz/15$\frac{1}{2}$-oz) can pineapple rings, drained
castor sugar to sprinkle

Place the flour, egg yolk, milk and water in the liquidiser and blend until smooth. Pour into a bowl.

Heat the oil in a deep fat pan to 180°C/360°F, or when a cube of day-old bread turns golden brown.

Whisk the egg white and fold into the batter. Dip the pineapple rings in the batter and coat evenly. Fry in the oil until golden brown. Drain on absorbent paper and sprinkle with castor sugar.

Serves 4

Apple-berry charlotte

METRIC/IMPERIAL/AMERICAN
1 kg/2 lb/2 lb cooking apples
lemon juice
225 g/8 oz/$\frac{1}{2}$ lb blackberries
50 g/2 oz/$\frac{1}{4}$ cup sugar
3 cloves
75 g/3 oz/2 slices white bread, crusts removed
50 g/2 oz/$\frac{1}{4}$ cup butter
25 g/1 oz/2 tablespoons demerara sugar

Peel and core the apples. Reserve three slices for decoration and sprinkle with a little lemon juice to prevent discoloration. Quarter the remaining apples.

Reserve a few blackberries for decoration and mix remainder with the quartered apples. Place in an ovenproof dish with the sugar and cloves.

Place the bread in the liquidiser and blend into fine breadcrumbs. Melt the butter in a frying pan and stir in the breadcrumbs; fry until golden. Mix with the demerara sugar and sprinkle over the fruit.

Bake in a moderately hot oven (190°C, 375°F, Gas Mark 5) for 35–45 minutes. Decorate with reserved slices of apple filled with the blackberries.

Serves 4–6

Pineapple meringue pie

METRIC/IMPERIAL/AMERICAN
mixer pastry (see page 20)
FILLING:
25 g/1 oz/2 tablespoons butter or margarine
25 g/1 oz/$\frac{1}{4}$ cup cornflour
1 (376-g/13$\frac{1}{4}$-oz/13$\frac{1}{4}$-oz) can pineapple pieces
50 g/2 oz/$\frac{1}{4}$ cup sugar
2 egg yolks
MERINGUE:
2 egg whites
75 g/3 oz/scant $\frac{1}{2}$ cup castor sugar
glacé cherries and angelica to decorate

Make the pastry and use to line a 20-cm/8-inch flan ring, placed on a baking sheet. Bake blind in a moderately hot oven (200°C, 400°F, Gas Mark 6) for 15 minutes. Reduce the oven temperature to moderate (180°C, 350°F, Gas Mark 4) and bake the flan for a further 10–15 minutes. Place the butter or margarine, cornflour, juice made up to 300 ml/$\frac{1}{2}$ pint/1$\frac{1}{4}$ cups, and the sugar in a saucepan. Whisking all the time, bring to the boil and cook for 2–3 minutes. Cool slightly. Beat in the egg yolks and fold in the drained pineapple pieces. Pour into the partly-cooked flan case. Place the egg whites in the mixer bowl and whisk until stiff. Add the sugar and whisk again until stiff. Pile on top of the pineapple mixture. Bake in a moderately hot oven (200°C, 400°F, Gas Mark 6) for 10–15 minutes. Decorate.

Serves 4–6

Brandied mincemeat soufflé

METRIC/IMPERIAL/AMERICAN
25 g/1 oz/2 tablespoons butter or margarine
50 g/2 oz/½ cup plain flour
150 ml/¼ pint/⅔ cup milk
25 g/1 oz/2 tablespoons castor sugar
3 egg yolks
1 tablespoon mincemeat
1 tablespoon brandy
3 egg whites
icing sugar to decorate

Place the butter, flour, milk and sugar in the liquidiser and switch on to maximum speed for 30 seconds. Pour into a saucepan and whisking all the time bring to the boil. Simmer gently for 1 minute, still stirring. Cool slightly.

Whisk the egg yolks into the cooled sauce. Fold in the mincemeat and brandy. Place the egg whites in the mixer bowl and whisk until stiff. Fold the whisked egg whites into the mincemeat mixture.

Pour into 4 individual greased soufflé dishes and cook in a moderately hot oven (190°C, 375°F, Gas Mark 5) for 40–45 minutes. Sprinkle with icing sugar and serve immediately with cream.

Serves 4

Fruity bakewell tart

METRIC/IMPERIAL/AMERICAN
ORANGE PASTRY:
100 g/4 oz/½ cup margarine
175 g/6 oz/1½ cups plain flour
grated rind of 1 orange
FILLING:
50 g/2 oz/¼ cup margarine
50 g/2 oz/½ cup ground almonds
100 g/4 oz/½ cup castor sugar
2 eggs
4–5 tablespoons/4–5 tablespoons/⅓ cup–6 tablespoons
   redcurrant jelly
2 bananas, sliced
angelica leaves to decorate

Place the margarine, 1 tablespoon water and one-third of the flour in the mixer bowl. Using a slow speed combine until just mixed. Add the remaining flour and the orange rind and mix again until a dough is formed. Knead lightly on a floured board. Roll out and line a 20-cm/8-inch flan ring placed on a baking sheet.

Place the margarine, ground almonds, sugar and eggs in the mixer bowl. Mix together on a slow speed until well mixed. Spread the redcurrant jelly over the base of the flan case. Arrange the bananas (reserving a few for decoration) on top and then cover with the almond mixture. Bake in a moderate oven (160°C, 325°F, Gas Mark 3) for 45–60 minutes. Decorate.

Serves 6

Mocha fudge pudding

METRIC/IMPERIAL/AMERICAN
75 g/3 oz/6 tablespoons soft margarine
50 g/2 oz/½ cup self-raising flour
25 g/1 oz/¼ cup cocoa powder
15 g/½ oz/2 tablespoons instant coffee granules
75 g/3 oz/6 tablespoons castor sugar
1 egg
50 g/2 oz/4 tablespoons brown sugar
40 g/1½ oz/scant ½ cup walnuts, chopped
SAUCE:
300 ml/½ pint/1¼ cups hot black coffee
50 g/2 oz/¼ cup castor sugar
DECORATION:
icing sugar
halved walnuts

Place the margarine, flour, half the cocoa powder, the coffee, sugar and egg in the mixer bowl and whisk on a slow speed until well mixed. Place in a 1-litre/2-pint ovenproof dish.

Sprinkle with the brown sugar, remaining cocoa powder and the walnuts. Mix the black coffee and sugar together and pour over. Bake in a moderate oven (160°C, 325°F, Gas Mark 3) for 50–60 minutes. Dredge with icing sugar, decorate with halved walnuts and serve with cream.

Serves 4–6

Gooseberry creams

METRIC/IMPERIAL/AMERICAN
1 kg/2 lb/2 lb gooseberries, topped and tailed
100 g/4 oz/½ cup castor sugar
green food colouring (optional)
½ teaspoon gelatine
1 tablespoon hot water
150 ml/¼ pint/⅔ cup double cream

Place the gooseberries and sugar in a saucepan and heat very gently until the sugar has dissolved. Pour into the liquidiser and blend into a purée. Add a few drops green colouring if liked.

Dissolve the gelatine in the water. Cool slightly, then stir into the gooseberry purée. Lightly whisk the cream and gently swirl into the gooseberry mixture. Chill and serve in individual glasses, with sponge finger biscuits.

Serves 6

Strawberry cream sorbet

METRIC/IMPERIAL/AMERICAN
350 g/12 oz/1¼ cups strawberries, hulled
50 g/2 oz/¼ cup castor sugar
1 (142-g/5-oz/5-oz) carton strawberry yogurt
few drops of lemon juice
150 ml/¼ pint/⅔ cup double cream
2 egg whites, whisked
DECORATION:
strawberries
mint leaves

Place the strawberries, sugar and yogurt in the liquidiser and blend until smooth. Add the lemon juice to taste.

Pour into a rigid polythene container and freeze for 1 hour. Turn out into a bowl and break up with a fork. Whisk the cream lightly and fold into the strawberry mixture with the whisked egg whites. Return to the freezer until firm. Spoon into glasses and decorate with strawberries and mint leaves.

Note: Raspberries may be substituted for strawberries.

Serves 4

Citrus cornflake freeze

METRIC/IMPERIAL/AMERICAN
75 g/3 oz/3 cups crushed cornflakes
25 g/1 oz/2 tablespoons castor sugar
25 g/1 oz/2 tablespoons butter, melted
2 eggs, separated
grated rind of 1 lemon
1 small can condensed milk
4 tablespoons/4 tablespoons/⅓ cup lemon juice
100 g/4 oz/½ cup castor sugar
slices of lemon to decorate

Mix together the crushed cornflakes, sugar and melted butter. Press half into the base of a 1-kg/2-lb loaf tin and chill.

Whisk the egg yolks until thick and creamy. Add the lemon rind, condensed milk and lemon juice and whisk until thickened.

Whisk the egg whites until stiff and fold in the sugar. Fold into the lemon mixture and pour on to the chilled cornflake base. Sprinkle the top with the remaining cornflakes. Freeze until firm. Carefully remove from the loaf tin and cut into slices. Decorate with slices of lemon.

Serves 4–6

Orange syllabub

METRIC/IMPERIAL/AMERICAN
300 ml/½ pint/1¼ cups double cream
2 tablespoons/2 tablespoons/3 tablespoons clear honey
2 tablespoons/2 tablespoons/3 tablespoons white wine
2 tablespoons/2 tablespoons/3 tablespoons fresh orange
   juice
finely grated rind of 1 orange
15 g/½ oz/1 tablespoon castor sugar

Place the cream, honey, wine, orange juice and half of the
orange rind in the mixer bowl and whisk until stiff. Spoon into
individual glasses and chill.

   Just before serving mix the remaining orange rind with the
sugar and sprinkle on top of the syllabub.

Serves 4

Blackberry meringue

METRIC/IMPERIAL/AMERICAN
4 egg whites
225 g/8 oz/1 cup castor sugar
CRÈME PATISSIÈRE:
25 g/1 oz/2 tablespoons butter
20 g/¾ oz/3 tablespoons plain flour
6 tablespoons/6 tablespoons/½ cup milk
25 g/1 oz/2 tablespoons castor sugar
1 egg yolk
1 tablespoon cream

225 g/8 oz/2 cups blackberries
150 ml/¼ pint/⅔ cup double cream, whipped

Place the egg whites in the mixer bowl and whisk until stiff.
Gradually add the sugar whisking all the time until stiff again.
Place the mixture in a piping bag fitted with a large star tube.
Line two baking sheets with silicone paper and pipe two circles,
20 cm/8 inches in diameter. Smooth evenly. Pipe the remaining
meringue into small rosettes. Bake in a cool oven (110°C, 225°F,
Gas Mark ¼) for 4–5 hours. Cool, then remove the paper.

   Place the butter, flour and milk in a saucepan and whisking all
the time over a moderate heat, bring to the boil. Cool slightly,
before whisking in the remaining ingredients. Allow to cool
completely, then sandwich the meringue circles together with
the crème patissière. Top with blackberries, piped cream and
meringue rosettes.

Serves 4–6

Strawberry cheesecake

METRIC/IMPERIAL/AMERICAN
100 g/4 oz/¼ lb digestive biscuits
50 g/2 oz/¼ cup butter, melted
FILLING:
225 g/8 oz/1 cup cream cheese
150 g/5 oz/generous ¼ cup natural yogurt
½ packet lemon jelly
3 tablespoons/3 tablespoons/¼ cup hot water
50 g/2 oz/¼ cup castor sugar
grated rind and juice of 1 lemon
DECORATION:
150 ml/¼ pint/⅔ cup double cream, whipped
few strawberries

Crush the digestive biscuits in the liquidiser. Place in a bowl and stir in the melted butter. Press into the base of a 20-cm/8-inch round loose-bottomed sandwich tin. Chill until firm.

Place the cheese and yogurt in the mixer bowl and whisk slowly until smooth. Dissolve the jelly in the water with the sugar and cool slightly. Pour into the cheese mixture together with the lemon rind and juice. Whisk on a slow speed until smooth. Pour over the biscuit base and chill until set. Carefully remove from the cake tin and decorate with piped cream and strawberries.

Serves 4–6

Coffee cream

METRIC/IMPERIAL/AMERICAN
3 teaspoons gelatine
3 tablespoons/3 tablespoons/¼ cup water
450 ml/¾ pint/2 cups double cream
150 ml/¼ pint/⅔ cup single cream
75 g/3 oz/6 tablespoons castor sugar
1 tablespoon instant coffee powder
2 teaspoons hot water
DECORATION:
150 ml/¼ pint/⅔ cup double cream, whipped
grated chocolate

Dissolve the gelatine in the water in a bowl placed over a saucepan of hot water. Place the double and single creams in the mixer bowl and whisk until the cream leaves a trail. Fold in the sugar. Dissolve the coffee powder in the hot water and stir into the dissolved gelatine and allow to cool slightly.

With the mixer at a medium speed pour in the dissolved coffee and gelatine. Whisk until the cream is on the point of setting. Pour into a rinsed out 1-litre/1 ¾-pint mould and chill. Turn out just before serving and decorate with whipped cream and grated chocolate.

Serves 4–6

Orange zabaglione

METRIC/IMPERIAL/AMERICAN
2 eggs
2 egg yolks
40 g/1½ oz/3 tablespoons castor sugar
grated rind and juice of 1 orange
2 tablespoons/2 tablespoons/3 tablespoons brandy

Place the eggs and yolks in bowl and whisk until combined.
Add the sugar and grated orange rind, place the bowl over a
saucepan of hot water and whisk until thick and frothy. Lastly,
whisk in the orange juice and brandy.

Pour into individual glasses and serve immediately.

Serves 6

Banana and blackcurrant fool

METRIC/IMPERIAL/AMERICAN
450 g/1 lb/4 cups blackcurrants, washed and hulled
2 tablespoons/2 tablespoons/3 tablespoons water
100 g/4 oz/½ cup castor sugar
2 bananas, sliced
300 ml/½ pint/1¼ cups double cream

Place the blackcurrants and water in a saucepan. Cover and
simmer for 10–15 minutes. Stir in the sugar and sliced bananas.
Place in the liquidiser and blend to a purée. Allow to cool.

Whip the cream and then fold in the fruit purée. Pour into a
serving dish or individual dishes and chill well.

Serves 4–6

Soured apricot fool

METRIC/IMPERIAL/AMERICAN
1 kg/2 lb/2 lb ripe apricots
3 tablespoons/3 tablespoons/¼ cup water
150 g/5 oz/⅔ cup castor sugar
grated rind of ½ orange
2 tablespoons/2 tablespoons/3 tablespoons orange juice
300 ml/½ pint/1¼ cups soured cream
DECORATION:
glacé cherries
angelica

Stone the apricots and place in a saucepan with the water and sugar. Bring to the boil and simmer gently until tender. Cool slightly, then place in the liquidiser and blend until smooth. Allow to cool.

Stir the orange rind and juice into the purée. Spoon into individual glasses with the soured cream. Swirl the purée and cream with a teaspoon. Chill well and decorate with a glacé cherry and angelica.

Serves 4–6

St Clements crunch flan

METRIC/IMPERIAL/AMERICAN
175 g/6 oz/⅓ lb chocolate digestive biscuits
50 g/2 oz/¼ cup butter, melted
grated rind of 1 orange
FILLING:
150 ml/¼ pint/⅔ cup double cream
1 small can condensed milk
3 tablespoons/3 tablespoons/¼ cup lemon juice
2 tablespoons/2 tablespoons/3 tablespoons orange juice
grated rind of 1 lemon

slices of orange to decorate

Place the digestive biscuits in the liquidiser and blend until crumbled. Place crumbs in a bowl and pour in the melted butter and orange rind. Mix well and line the base and sides of six individual dishes or a 20-cm/8-inch flan dish, using the back of a metal spoon. Chill well.

Lightly whisk the cream and fold in the condensed milk, lemon juice, orange juice and lemon rind. Pour into the chilled biscuit shell. Chill until set.

Decorate with slices of orange.

Serves 6

Apricot sherbet

METRIC/IMPERIAL/AMERICAN
1 (411-g/14½-oz/14½-oz) can apricots, drained
2 eggs, separated
25 g/1 oz/2 tablespoons castor sugar
25 g/1 oz/¼ cup ground almonds
4 tablespoons/4 tablespoons/⅓ cup cream

Place apricots in the liquidiser and blend to a purée. Place the
egg whites in the mixer bowl and whisk until stiff. Whisk in the
sugar.

Combine the egg yolks, ground almonds and cream. Fold
into the egg whites together with the apricot purée. Pour into a
shallow rigid polythene container and freeze for 4 hours, or
until hard. Scoop out with a spoon into serving dishes.

Serves 4

Blackberry flummery

METRIC/IMPERIAL/AMERICAN
450 g/1 lb/4 cups blackberries
600 ml/1 pint/2½ cups water
2 teaspoons cornflour
100 g/4 oz/½ cup castor sugar
1 tablespoon lemon juice
2 eggs
150 ml/¼ pint/⅔ cup double cream

Place the blackberries (reserving a few for decoration) and
water in a saucepan. Bring to the boil, then simmer gently until
tender. Allow to cool slightly then place in the liquidiser and
blend to a purée.

Mix the cornflour with a little of the purée until smooth.
Place the remaining purée in a saucepan, add the sugar and
bring to the boil. Stir in the blended cornflour and lemon juice.
Return to the heat and stir until thick. Cool.

Separate eggs and add the yolks to the cooled purée. Place the
egg whites in mixer bowl and whisk until fairly stiff. Fold into
the blackberry purée. Pour into individual dishes. Whip the
cream lightly and swirl into the purée. Serve decorated with the
reserved blackberries.

Serves 4–6

Gingered pear flan

METRIC/IMPERIAL/AMERICAN
225 g/8 oz/½ lb ginger biscuits
75 g/3 oz/6 tablespoons butter, melted
FILLING:
25 g/1 oz/2 tablespoons butter
25 g/1 oz/¼ cup plain flour
100 ml/4 fl oz/½ cup milk
1 egg yolk
25 g/1 oz/2 tablespoons sugar
grated rind of 1 orange
1 tablespoon cream
1 tablespoon brandy
1 (411-g/14½-oz/14½-oz) can pear halves, drained
2 oranges, peeled and segmented
DECORATION:
whipped cream
angelica leaves

Roughly break up the ginger biscuits, then crush them in the liquidiser. Place in a bowl and mix with the melted butter. Press into the base and sides of a 20-cm/8-inch flan dish or shallow pie dish, using the back of a metal spoon. Chill.

Place the butter, flour and milk in a saucepan and whisking continuously bring to the boil. Cool slightly then whisk in the egg yolk, sugar, orange rind, cream and brandy. Pour into the biscuit shell. Arrange the pears and orange segments on top of the filling. Decorate with cream and angelica.

Serves 6

Normandy flan

METRIC/IMPERIAL/AMERICAN
mixer pastry (see page 20)
450 g/1 lb/1 lb cooking apples, peeled, cored and sliced
1 tablespoon water
75 g/3 oz/6 tablespoons sugar
50 g/2 oz/¼ cup butter
2 egg yolks
grated rind of 1 orange
2 red-skinned eating apples
sieved apricot jam to glaze
icing sugar to sprinkle

Make the pastry and use to line a 20-cm/8-inch flan dish. Bake blind in a moderately hot oven (200°C, 400°F, Gas Mark 6) for 15 minutes. Reduce the oven temperature to moderate (180°C, 350°F, Gas Mark 4) and continue to cook the flan for a further 10–15 minutes. Cool.

Cook the apples with the water and sugar until soft. Whisk into a purée. Remove from the heat and beat in the butter, egg yolks and orange rind. Pour into the flan case.

Slice the eating apples, leaving the skin on and arrange on top of the apple purée. Brush with apricot jam and return to a moderately hot oven (200°C, 400°F, Gas Mark 6) for 25 minutes. Dredge the surface of the flan with icing sugar and place under a hot grill to caramelise the apples. Serve cold with cream.

Serves 4–6

Citrus crunch pie

METRIC/IMPERIAL/AMERICAN
150 g/5 oz/5 oz semi-sweet biscuits
100 g/4 oz/½ cup butter, melted
100 g/4 oz/½ cup castor sugar
FILLING:
2 eggs, separated
100 g/4 oz/½ cup castor sugar
grated rind and juice of 1 small lemon
1 teaspoon gelatine
pinch cream of tartar
4 tablespoons/4 tablespoons/⅓ cup double cream
whipped cream and slices of lemon to decorate

Place the biscuits in the liquidiser and blend into fine crumbs.
Mix with the melted butter and sugar. Press the mixture over
the base and sides of a greased 20-cm/8-inch flan dish. Chill.

Place the egg yolks, half the sugar, the lemon rind and juice in
a bowl placed over a saucepan of hot water, and whisk until
thick and creamy. Dissolve the gelatine in 1 tablespoon hot
water then stir into the egg mixture; cool.

Place the egg whites in the mixer bowl and whisk with the
cream of tartar until foamy. Add the remaining sugar and whisk
until stiff. Whisk the cream until thick. When the egg mixture
begins to set, whisk lightly until smooth, then fold in the egg
whites and cream. Pour into the biscuit base and chill. Decorate.

Serves 4–6

Banana ice cream

METRIC/IMPERIAL/AMERICAN
100 g/4 oz/½ cup granulated sugar
300 ml/½ pint/1¼ cups water
300 ml/½ pint/1¼ cups banana purée (made in the
    liquidiser using 5 ripe bananas)
grated rind of ½ lemon
1 egg white
150 ml/¼ pint/⅔ cup double cream

Place the sugar and water in a saucepan and dissolve over a low
heat. Bring to the boil and cook quickly for 10 minutes. Allow
to become quite cold. Stir the banana purée into the syrup and
pour into a shallow rigid container and freeze until semi-solid.

Remove from the freezer and beat with an electric whisk until
smooth. Stir in the lemon rind. Place the egg white in the mixer
bowl and whisk until stiff. Fold into the banana mixture. Return
the mixture to the container and freeze again until semi-solid.
Beat again with the electric whisk. Whisk the cream lightly and
fold into the banana ice cream. Freeze again until firm.

Allow to soften slightly for 30 minutes in the refrigerator
before serving. Serve topped with slices of banana, dipped in
lemon juice.

Serves 4–6

Cakes, teabreads and cookies

In this chapter the mixer really comes into its own, taking all the hard work out of creaming and beating. Simply place all the ingredients in the mixer bowl and combine together – what could be quicker and easier!

Meringues and whisked sponges are effortless to make in the mixer.

Most cakes, teabreads and cookies freeze well, preferably un-iced. Batch baking becomes really speedy with the combination of a mixer and freezer.

Coffee almond gâteau

METRIC/IMPERIAL/AMERICAN

4 eggs
4 tablespoons/4 tablespoons/$\frac{1}{3}$ cup coffee essence
100 g/4 oz/$\frac{1}{2}$ cup castor sugar
75 g/3 oz/$\frac{3}{4}$ cup plain flour
25 g/1 oz/$\frac{1}{4}$ cup cornflour
225 g/8 oz/1 cup butter or margarine
275 g/10 oz/$2\frac{1}{4}$ cups icing sugar
100 g/4 oz/1 cup flaked almonds, toasted
icing sugar

Place the eggs, half the coffee essence and the castor sugar in the mixer bowl (or if using a hand whisk, place in a bowl over a saucepan of hot water). Whisk until thick and creamy. If whisking over hot water, remove from the heat when thick and continue whisking for a few minutes. Sieve the flour and cornflour over the mixture and fold in. Pour into two 20-cm/8-inch greased and lined sandwich tins. Bake in a moderately hot oven (190°C, 375°F, Gas Mark 5) for 25–30 minutes. Cool on a wire tray.

Place the butter or margarine in the mixer bowl and gradually whisk in the sieved icing sugar with the remaining coffee essence. Sandwich the cakes together with a little of the icing. Spread the remainder over the sides and top. Press the toasted almonds all over the cake. Cut four 2.5-cm/1-inch wide strips of greaseproof paper and lay them across the top of the cake, leaving a gap between each. Dredge with icing sugar, then carefully lift off.

Tipsy coffee ring cake

METRIC/IMPERIAL/AMERICAN
100 g/4 oz/½ cup butter or margarine
100 g/4 oz/½ cup castor sugar
2 eggs
100 g/4 oz/1 cup self-raising flour
grated rind of 1 orange
1 tablespoon coffee essence
SYRUP:
100 g/4 oz/½ cup castor sugar
juice of 2 oranges, strained
1–2 teaspoons Tia Maria or sherry
150 ml/¼ pint/⅔ cup double cream to decorate

Place the butter or margarine and sugar in the mixer bowl and beat until light and fluffy. Beat in the eggs one at a time, adding a little flour with the second egg. Using a metal spoon fold in the remaining flour. Divide the mixture in two. Add the orange rind to one half and coffee essence to the other. Place alternate spoonfuls of the mixtures in a greased fluted or plain ring mould. Swirl with a skewer to give a marbled effect.

Bake in a moderate oven (180°C, 350°F, Gas Mark 4) for 40–50 minutes. Turn out and cool on a wire tray.

Dissolve the sugar and orange juice in a saucepan over a low heat. Add the Tia Maria or sherry. Make holes in the base of the cake with a skewer and pour over the syrup until it is all absorbed.

Whisk the cream and pipe rosettes around the cake.

Rich fruit cake

METRIC/IMPERIAL/AMERICAN
150 g/5 oz/generous ½ cup butter or margarine
175 g/6 oz/¾ cup soft brown sugar
1 tablespoon black treacle
4 eggs
200 g/7 oz/1¾ cups plain flour
275 g/10 oz/2 cups currants
200 g/7 oz/generous 1 cup sultanas
65 g/2½ oz/generous ¼ cup glacé cherries, chopped
65 g/2½ oz/⅔ cup almonds, chopped
65 g/2½ oz/generous ¼ cup mixed peel
1 teaspoon mixed spice
½ teaspoon nutmeg
grated rind and juice of 1 orange
50 g/2 oz/½ cup ground almonds

Place the butter or margarine and sugar in the mixer bowl and beat until well creamed. Beat in the treacle, then add the eggs gradually, adding a little flour with each egg after the first. Fold in the remaining ingredients. Place in a greased and lined 20-cm/8-inch round or 18-cm/7-inch square cake tin. Smooth the top. Bake in a cool oven (140°C, 275°F, Gas Mark 1). Test the cake after the first 3 hours with a skewer. If it is not cooked check at 30-minute intervals. The cake is cooked when the skewer is no longer sticky. Leave to cool in the tin for 15 minutes before cooling on a wire tray.

Devil's food cake

METRIC/IMPERIAL/AMERICAN
CAKE:
100 g/4 oz/½ cup margarine
150 g/5 oz/⅔ cup castor sugar
3 eggs
150 g/5 oz/1¼ cups self-raising flour
1 teaspoon baking powder
3 tablespoons/3 tablespoons/¼ cup cocoa powder
2 teaspoons orange juice
100 g/4 oz/1 cup ground almonds
150 ml/¼ pint/⅔ cup natural yogurt
ICING:
75 g/3 oz/6 tablespoons margarine
225 g/8 oz/scant 2 cups icing sugar, sieved
1–2 tablespoons/1–2 tablespoons/1–3 tablespoons orange
   juice
circles of chocolate to decorate (see method)

Place all the cake ingredients in the mixer bowl and using a slow speed combine together. Place the mixture in three greased and lined 18-cm/7-inch sandwich cake tins. Bake in the centre of a very moderate oven (160°C, 325°F, Gas Mark 3) for 25–35 minutes. Cool on a wire tray.

Place icing ingredients in the mixer bowl and mix until smooth. Sandwich the cakes together with some icing. Spread some icing over the top and use the remainder to pipe a border. Decorate with circles of chocolate. To make these, spread melted chocolate over a sheet of waxed paper. Allow to set, then cut out circles using a small fluted cutter.

Strawberry gâteau

METRIC/IMPERIAL/AMERICAN
SPONGE BASE:
4 eggs
100 g/4 oz/½ cup castor sugar
100 g/4 oz/1 cup plain flour
¾ teaspoon baking powder
FILLING:
3 tablespoons/3 tablespoons/¼ cup strawberry jam
225 g/8 oz/2 cups strawberries
300 ml/½ pint/1¼ cups double cream, whipped
icing sugar to sprinkle

Place the eggs and sugar in the mixer bowl (or if using a hand whisk, place in a bowl over a saucepan of hot water). Whisk until thick and creamy and the mixture leaves a trail. If whisking over hot water, remove from the heat when thick and whisk for a few minutes to allow the mixture to cool. Sieve the flour and baking powder and carefully fold into the whisked mixture.

Line the bases of two 20-cm/8-inch sandwich tins, grease and dust with a little flour. Pour the mixture into the tins. Bake in a moderate oven (180°C, 350°F, Gas Mark 4) for 25–35 minutes. Turn out and cool on a wire tray. Cut one of the sponges into six wedges. Spread the jam over the uncut sponge with some sliced strawberries and a little whipped cream. Carefully arrange the wedges on the top to form a circle and sprinkle with sieved icing sugar. Pipe with cream and decorate with strawberries.

44

Mocha gâteau

METRIC/IMPERIAL/AMERICAN
CAKE:
175 g/6 oz/¾ cup butter or margarine
175 g/6 oz/¾ cup castor sugar
3 eggs
175 g/6 oz/1½ cups self-raising flour, sieved
1 tablespoon cocoa powder, sieved
ICING:
350 g/12 oz/2⅔ cups icing sugar, sieved
140 g/4½ oz/generous ½ cup butter or margarine
2 tablespoons/2 tablespoons/3 tablespoons milk
1 tablespoon coffee essence
browned flaked almonds to decorate

Place the butter or margarine and sugar in the mixer bowl and
cream together until light and fluffy. Beat in the eggs one at a
time adding a little of the flour with each egg after the first.
Using a metal spoon fold in the flour and cocoa powder. Place
the mixture in two greased and lined 18-cm/7-inch sandwich
tins. Bake in a moderate oven (160°C, 325°F, Gas Mark 3) for
25–35 minutes. Turn out and cool on a wire tray.

To make the icing, place all the ingredients in the mixer bowl
and using a slow speed combine until smooth.

Split each cake in half horizontally and sandwich the layers
together with a little of the icing. Spread some icing around the
sides and roll in the browned almonds. Use the remaining icing
to spread over the top of the cake and pipe rosettes around the
edge and on the top.

Fruit 'n' nut cake

METRIC/IMPERIAL/AMERICAN
100 g/4 oz/½ cup butter or margarine, softened
100 g/4 oz/½ cup castor sugar
2 eggs
grated rind of 1 orange
150 g/5 oz/1¼ cups plain flour
½ teaspoon nutmeg
100 g/4 oz/⅔ cup raisins
25 g/1 oz/3 tablespoons chopped angelica
100 g/4 oz/1 cup glacé cherries, halved
50 g/2 oz/½ cup brazil nuts, chopped
50 g/2 oz/½ cup almonds, chopped
50 g/2 oz/½ cup walnuts, chopped
1–2 tablespoons/1–2 tablespoons/1–3 tablespoons orange
   juice
DECORATION:
glacé cherries
whole brazil nuts
pieces of angelica
apricot jam

Place all the ingredients in the mixer bowl and using a slow
speed gradually combine until well mixed. Place in a greased
and lined 15-cm/6-inch round cake tin. Smooth top with the
back of a spoon or palette knife. Arrange circles of cherries,
brazil nuts and angelica on top. Bake in a cool oven (140°C,
275°F, Gas Mark 1) for 2½–3 hours. Turn out on to a wire tray
and brush the topping with a little heated apricot jam to glaze.
Allow to cool before serving.

Coffee meringues

METRIC/IMPERIAL/AMERICAN
3 egg whites
150 g/6 oz/$\frac{3}{4}$ cup castor sugar
1 tablespoon coffee essence
300 ml/$\frac{1}{2}$ pint/1$\frac{1}{4}$ cups double cream
1–2 tablespoons/1–2 tablespoons/1–3 tablespoons brandy
    (optional)
DECORATION:
glacé cherries, chopped
angelica

Line two to three baking sheets with silicone paper. Place the egg whites in the mixing bowl and whisk until stiff. Add the sugar gradually, whisking all the time until stiff. Fold in the coffee essence.

Place the meringue in a piping bag fitted with a large star piping tube. Pipe stars on to the lined baking sheets. Bake in a very cool oven (110°C, 200°F, Gas Mark $\frac{1}{4}$) for 3–4 hours. Allow to cool on a wire tray.

Whisk the cream lightly, adding the brandy if used. Sandwich the meringues together in pairs with the cream and decorate with the cherries and angelica.

Illustrated on the cover

Wiltshire teabread

METRIC/IMPERIAL/AMERICAN
275 g/10 oz/2$\frac{1}{2}$ cups plain flour
1 teaspoon mixed spice
1 teaspoon bicarbonate of soda
100 g/4 oz/$\frac{1}{2}$ cup soft margarine
150 ml/$\frac{1}{4}$ pint/$\frac{2}{3}$ cup milk
1 tablespoon lemon juice
100 g/4 oz/$\frac{1}{2}$ cup soft brown sugar
100 g/4 oz/$\frac{2}{3}$ cup sultanas
100 g/4 oz/$\frac{2}{3}$ cup currants
grated rind of 1 lemon
1 egg

Place all the ingredients in the mixer bowl and using a slow speed mix until a dropping consistency is obtained. Cover and leave overnight.

Place the mixture in a 450-g/1-lb greased and lined loaf tin, smoothing the surface with a knife. Bake in a moderate oven (160°C, 325°F, Gas Mark 3) for 2 hours. Allow to cool in the tin before turning out.

Serve sliced and spread with butter.

Gingerbread loaf

METRIC/IMPERIAL/AMERICAN
175 g/6 oz/¾ cup butter
75 g/3 oz/6 tablespoons soft brown sugar
75 g/3 oz/¼ cup black treacle
3 eggs
225 g/8 oz/2 cups self-raising flour
1 tablespoon/1 tablespoon/1 tablespoon ground ginger
3 pieces stem ginger, fincly chopped
25 g/1 oz/¼ cup flaked almonds

Place the butter, sugar and treacle in the mixer bowl and mix until light and fluffy. Add the eggs, beating well on a medium speed. Using a metal spoon fold in the flour, ground and stem ginger. Place in a greased and lined 1-kg/2-lb loaf tin. Sprinkle the flaked almonds over the surface, then bake in a moderate oven (180°C, 350°F, Gas Mark 4) for 1–1¼ hours. Turn out and cool on a wire tray.

Serve sliced and spread with butter.

Banana teabread

METRIC/IMPERIAL/AMERICAN
450 g/1 lb/1 lb ripe bananas
100 g/4 oz/½ cup butter or margarine
150 g/6 oz/¾ cup castor sugar
2 eggs
225 g/8 oz/2 cups self-raising flour
grated rind of 1 lemon
50 g/2 oz/¼ cup glacé cherries, chopped
100 g/4 oz/⅔ cup raisins

Mash the bananas, reserving a whole one for decoration. Place all the ingredients in the mixer bowl and beat slowly until well mixed. Place in a 1-kg/2-lb greased and lined loaf tin.

Bake in a moderate oven (160°C, 325°F, Gas Mark 3) for 1½–1¾ hours. Turn out and cool on a wire tray. Decorate with the reserved banana cut into slices and dipped in lemon juice. Slice and spread with butter.

Malted apricot and walnut teabread

METRIC/IMPERIAL/AMERICAN
75 g/3 oz/4½ tablespoons malt extract
50 g/2 oz/4 tablespoons soft brown sugar
25 g/1 oz/2 tablespoons margarine
225 g/8 oz/2 cups plain wholemeal flour
2 teaspoons baking powder
50 g/2 oz/½ cup walnuts, chopped
50 g/2 oz/6 tablespoons sultanas
25 g/1 oz/3 tablespoons dried apricots, chopped
grated rind of 1 orange
150 ml/¼ pint/⅔ cup milk
halved walnuts for topping

Melt the malt extract, sugar and margarine and allow to cool slightly. Place remaining dry ingredients in the mixer bowl and pour in the melted ingredients together with the milk. Mix on a slow speed until well combined. Place in a greased and lined 450-g/1-lb loaf tin. Lightly press halved walnuts over the top of the loaf. Bake in a moderate oven (160°C, 325°F, Gas Mark 3) for 1¼–1½ hours. Turn out and cool on a wire tray. Serve sliced and spread with butter.

Nutty cheese scone round

METRIC/IMPERIAL/AMERICAN
225 g/8 oz/2 cups self-raising flour
pinch dry mustard
salt and pepper
40 g/1½ oz/3 tablespoons butter or margarine
25 g/1 oz/¼ cup walnuts, finely chopped
75 g/3 oz/¾ cup cheese, finely grated
7 tablespoons/7 tablespoons/generous ½ cup milk
milk to glaze
few chopped or ground walnuts to decorate

Place all the ingredients, except the milk, in the mixer bowl. Using a slow speed gradually pour in the milk until the mixture forms a soft dough.

Turn out on to a lightly floured board and knead gently. Roll out into a 20-cm/8-inch round and score into eight sections using a sharp knife. Brush with milk and sprinkle with walnuts. Bake in a hot oven (220°C, 425°F, Gas Mark 7) for 15–20 minutes.

Serve hot or cold with butter.

Cheese and herb loaf

METRIC/IMPERIAL/AMERICAN
50 g/2 oz/¼ cup soft margarine
150 ml/¼ pint/⅔ cup milk
1 egg
75 g/3 oz/¾ cup Cheddar cheese, grated
225 g/8 oz/2 cups self-raising flour
1 teaspoon baking powder
pinch dry mustard
1 tablespoon chopped parsley
½ teaspoon chervil
parsley sprigs to garnish

Place all the ingredients in the mixer bowl and using a slow
speed, beat until well mixed. Place the mixture in a greased and
lined 450-g/1-lb loaf tin. Smooth the top. Bake in a moderate
oven (180°C, 350°F, Gas Mark 4) for 1–1¼ hours. Turn out and
serve either hot or cold. Garnish with parsley sprigs.
Note: Sliced and spread with butter, this loaf makes an ideal
base for open sandwiches.

Grannie's cookies

METRIC/IMPERIAL/AMERICAN
100 g/4 oz/½ cup butter
350 g/12 oz/1½ cups castor sugar
1 large egg
250 g/9 oz/2¼ cups self-raising flour
1 teaspoon ground ginger
pinch ground nutmeg

Place the butter and sugar in the mixer bowl and beat until soft
and well combined. Beat in the egg. Using a metal spoon stir in
the flour, ginger and nutmeg. Place on a board and knead into a
firm dough. Roll into balls the size of a walnut. Place on greased
baking sheets, keeping well apart. Bake in a cool oven (150°C,
300°F, Gas Mark 2) for 30–40 minutes. Cool on a wire tray.

Makes approximately 30

Viennese biscuits

METRIC/IMPERIAL/AMERICAN
225 g/8 oz/1 cup margarine
75 g/3 oz/¾ cup icing sugar, sieved
grated rind of 1 lemon
200 g/7 oz/1¾ cups plain flour
50 g/2 oz/½ cup cornflour
ICING:
225 g/8 oz/2 cups icing sugar, sieved
75 g/3 oz/6 tablespoons margarine
2 teaspoons lemon juice
100 g/4 oz/4 squares chocolate, melted, to decorate

Place the margarine and icing sugar in the mixer bowl and beat together until light and creamy. Beat in the lemon rind, flour and cornflour and mix to a soft paste. Put the mixture in a piping bag fitted with a large star tube and pipe into fingers on a greased baking sheet, 2.5 cm/1 inch apart. Bake in a moderately hot oven (190°C, 375°F, Gas Mark 5) for 15–20 minutes. Cool on a wire tray.

To make the icing, place all the ingredients in the mixer bowl and using a slow speed gradually combine until the mixture is light and creamy.

Sandwich the biscuits together in pairs with the icing and dip the ends into the melted chocolate. Leave to set.

Makes 12–14 pairs

Butterscotch brownies

METRIC/IMPERIAL/AMERICAN
100 g/4 oz/½ cup butter or margarine
175 g/6 oz/¾ cup soft brown sugar
2 eggs
50 g/2 oz/½ cup walnuts, chopped
75 g/3 oz/¾ cup self-raising flour
¼ teaspoon baking powder
40 g/1½ oz/¾ cup cocoa powder
DECORATION:
icing sugar
walnut halves

Place all the ingredients in the mixer bowl and beat until well mixed. Place in a lined and greased 18-cm/7-inch square cake tin. Bake in a moderate oven (180°C, 350°F, Gas Mark 4) for 40–50 minutes. Turn out and cool on a wire tray.

Dredge with icing sugar and then cut into squares. Place a walnut half on each square.

Oatcakes

METRIC/IMPERIAL/AMERICAN
75 g/3 oz/6 tablespoons butter or margarine
100 g/4 oz/1 cup self-raising flour
pinch salt
100 g/4 oz/1 generous cup rolled oats
25 g/1 oz/2 tablespoons castor sugar
1 egg, beaten
1 teaspoon milk

Place the butter or margarine, flour, salt, oats and sugar in the mixer bowl. Using a slow speed mix the ingredients until just combined. Pour in the egg and milk and mix into a stiff dough. Turn on to a floured board and knead lightly.

Roll out thinly and cut out circles using a 6-cm/2½-inch plain cutter. Place on a greased baking sheet and prick lightly with a fork. Bake in a moderate oven (180°C, 350°F, Gas Mark 4) for 15–20 minutes. Cool on a wire tray and serve with cheese.

Macaroons

METRIC/IMPERIAL/AMERICAN
100 g/4 oz/½ cup castor sugar
100 g/4 oz/1 cup ground almonds
1 teaspoon ground rice
2 egg whites
few drops of almond essence
halved almonds

Place the sugar, ground almonds and ground rice in the mixer bowl and using a slow speed gradually beat in the egg whites and almond essence until the mixture is of a soft piping consistency. Place in a piping bag fitted with a 1-cm/½-inch plain tube. Pipe the mixture into 3.5–5-cm/1½–2-inch circles on rice paper placed on baking sheets. Press a halved almond into each macaroon. Bake in a moderate oven (160°C, 325°F, Gas Mark 3) for 15–20 minutes. Using a palette knife place the macaroons on a wire tray to cool.

Makes 20–24

Crispy peanut cookies

METRIC/IMPERIAL/AMERICAN
100 g/4 oz/½ cup soft margarine
100 g/4 oz/½ cup soft brown sugar
100 g/4 oz/1 cup salted peanuts
4 teaspoons coffee essence
150 g/5 oz/1¼ cups self-raising flour
¼ teaspoon cinnamon

Place all the ingredients in the mixer bowl and mix until a soft dough is formed. Roll into balls the size of a walnut. Place well apart on greased baking trays. Flatten each cookie with the back of a fork. Bake in a moderate oven (180°C, 350°F, Gas Mark 4) for 10–12 minutes. Cool on a wire tray.

If liked, sandwich the cookies in pairs with peanut butter.

Makes approximately 25–30

Orange shortbread

METRIC/IMPERIAL/AMERICAN
100 g/4 oz/½ cup butter
50 g/2 oz/¼ cup castor sugar
175 g/6 oz/1½ cups plain flour
grated rind of 1 orange
DECORATION:
castor sugar
orange segments

Place all the ingredients in the mixer bowl and using a slow speed combine them until sticky. Spoon into a 20-cm/8-inch round flan ring placed on a baking sheet. Press down using the back of a tablespoon to smooth the surface. Prick lightly with a fork and divide into portions marking halfway through the shortbread with a sharp knife. Bake in a cool oven (150°C, 300°F, Gas Mark 2) for 40–50 minutes. Remove the flan ring carefully and cool the shortbread on a wire tray.

Dredge the shortbread with castor sugar and decorate with orange segments.

Sauces and dressings

Sauces and dressings add the finishing touch to many dishes and are so easy to make with a liquidiser.

You can make a basic white sauce in seconds without the agony of wondering if it will turn out lumpy! A sauce usually has to be made at the last minute, but with your liquidiser you can combine all the ingredients in the goblet in advance and then leave in the saucepan until ready to heat and serve.

Mayonnaise and Hollandaise sauce are often thought to be difficult to make but, with the aid of your appliances, you can be sure of a perfect result every time.

White sauce

METRIC/IMPERIAL/AMERICAN
25 g/1 oz/2 tablespoons butter
25 g/1 oz/¼ cup flour
300 ml/½ pint/1¼ cups milk
salt and pepper

Place all the ingredients in the liquidiser and switch on to maximum speed for 30 seconds. Pour the mixture into a saucepan and whisking all the time bring to the boil. Simmer gently for 1 minute, still stirring. Serve as an accompaniment to vegetable dishes.

Variations
Béchamel sauce: Place the milk in a saucepan with 1 carrot, 1 onion, 1 bay leaf and pinch of nutmeg. Bring to the boil, remove from the heat and infuse for 30 minutes. Strain milk and use to make basic white sauce as above.
Cheese sauce: Stir 50 g/2 oz/½ cup grated cheese and a pinch of mustard into the cooked sauce. Do not allow to boil once the cheese has been added.
Mushroom sauce: Stir 50 g/2 oz/½ cup chopped sautéed mushrooms into the cooked sauce.
Parsley sauce: Stir 3 tablespoons/3 tablespoons/¼ cup chopped parsley into the cooked sauce.
Anchovy sauce: Stir 2–3 teaspoons anchovy essence and a few drops of lemon juice into the cooked sauce.

Makes 300 ml/½ pint/1¼ cups

Tomato sauce

METRIC/IMPERIAL/AMERICAN
50 g/2 oz/¼ cup butter or margarine
1 rasher bacon, derinded and chopped
2 onions, chopped
450 g/1 lb/1 lb tomatoes, roughly chopped
1 clove garlic, crushed
bouquet garni
pinch sugar
salt and pepper
few parsley sprigs
few drops of Worcestershire sauce

Melt the butter or margarine and sauté the bacon, onions and tomatoes for 10 minutes in a covered pan, shaking occasionally.

Add the remaining ingredients and simmer gently for 30 minutes. Remove the bouquet garni. Pour into the liquidiser and blend until smooth. Sieve and return to a clean saucepan and reheat. Serve with spaghetti or other pasta.

Serves 4–6

Barbecue sauce

METRIC/IMPERIAL/AMERICAN
1 onion, chopped
2 sticks celery, chopped
1 clove garlic, crushed
150 ml/¼ pint/⅔ cup water
300 ml/½ pint/1¼ cups red wine
1 tablespoon wine vinegar
1 tablespoon brown sugar
few drops of Tabasco sauce
1 tablespoon Worcestershire sauce
2 tablespoons/2 tablespoons/3 tablespoons redcurrant
    jelly
salt
freshly ground black pepper
1 tablespoon cornflour blended in a little water

Place all the ingredients except the blended cornflour in a saucepan and bring to the boil. Simmer for 10 minutes and then allow to cool slightly.

Pour into the liquidiser and blend until smooth. Return to the saucepan, stir in the blended cornflour and heat until thickened.

Serve as an accompaniment to kebabs, ham, pork or lamb dishes.

Serves 4

Hollandaise sauce

METRIC/IMPERIAL/AMERICAN
225 g/8 oz/1 cup butter
1 tablespoon water
4 egg yolks
2 tablespoons/2 tablespoons/3 tablespoons lemon juice
freshly ground black pepper
pinch cayenne pepper
salt to taste

Melt the butter in the water in a saucepan, but do not allow to brown. Place the egg yolks, lemon juice, black pepper and cayenne pepper in the liquidiser. Turn on to the slowest speed and pour in the melted butter mixture in a steady stream, until the sauce has emulsified. Add salt to taste.
  Serve cold with fish and vegetable dishes.

Serves 4

Cranberry sauce

METRIC/IMPERIAL/AMERICAN
225 g/8 oz/2 cups cranberries
100 g/4 oz/½ cup sugar
3 tablespoons/3 tablespoons/¼ cup water
grated rind of ½ lemon

Place the cranberries, sugar, water and lemon rind in a saucepan and bring to the boil. Simmer for 10–15 minutes. Allow to cool slightly.
  Pour into the liquidiser and blend until smooth.
  Chill before serving as an accompaniment to poultry and game dishes.

Serves 4

Mixer mayonnaise

METRIC/IMPERIAL/AMERICAN
2 egg yolks
pinch dry mustard
salt and pepper
pinch castor sugar
300 ml/$\frac{1}{2}$ pint/$1\frac{1}{4}$ cups oil
1–2 tablespoons/1–2 tablespoons/1–3 tablespoons wine
    vinegar or lemon juice

Place the egg yolks, mustard, seasoning and sugar in the mixer bowl and whisk gently until combined. Continue whisking and gradually pour the oil in drop by drop. When thick and smooth add the wine vinegar or lemon juice to thin the mayonnaise to the required consistency.
Note: If making mayonnaise in the liquidiser use 1 whole egg in place of the 2 egg yolks. Place the whole egg, seasonings and half the vinegar or lemon juice in the liquidiser and switch on at a slow speed. Pour the oil in a thin stream until the mixture begins to thicken, add the remaining vinegar or lemon juice. Then add any remaining oil, increasing the speed.
    When making mayonnaise, have all the ingredients at room temperature.

Garlic mayonnaise: Add 1 crushed clove of garlic to the mayonnaise.
Herb mayonnaise: Add 2 tablespoons/2 tablespoons/3 tablespoons chopped parsley or chives.
Mayonnaise verte: Add $\frac{1}{2}$ bunch finely chopped watercress just before serving.

French dressing

METRIC/IMPERIAL/AMERICAN
300 ml/$\frac{1}{2}$ pint/$1\frac{1}{4}$ cups oil
3 tablespoons/3 tablespoons/$\frac{1}{4}$ cup wine vinegar
pinch sugar
salt and pepper
pinch paprika pepper
pinch mixed herbs

Place all the ingredients in the liquidiser and blend until an emulsion is formed. Store in an airtight bottle in a cool place and shake well before using.

Variations
Garlic dressing: Keep 1 peeled clove of garlic in dressing; this will impart a delicate flavour.
Orange dressing: Add the grated rind of $\frac{1}{2}$ orange to the dressing.
Parsley dressing: Before blending add several sprigs of parsley to the dressing.

Blue cheese dressing

METRIC/IMPERIAL/AMERICAN
100 g/4 oz/½ cup blue cheese, crumbled
175 g/6 oz/¾ cup cream or curd cheese
150 ml/¼ pint/⅔ cup milk
1 teaspoon grated onion
salt
freshly ground black pepper
few parsley sprigs

Place all the ingredients in the liquidiser and blend until smooth.
    Serve with tomato or cucumber salad, or hamburgers.

Serves 4

Cucumber dressing

METRIC/IMPERIAL/AMERICAN
½ cucumber
few fresh mint leaves
few drops of lemon juice
salt
freshly ground black pepper
150 ml/¼ pint/⅔ cup soured cream

Cut the peeled cucumber into chunks and place in the liquidiser with the mint leaves and lemon juice. Blend until smooth. Mix in the seasoning and soured cream. Serve with salads, fish or chicken dishes.

Serves 4

Drinks

A wide range of drinks can be made with the aid of your liquidiser.

Some of the larger liquidisers will crush ice in seconds. You can also colour sugar to decorate the rims of glasses by adding a couple of drops of food colouring to granulated sugar. Blend until the colour is distributed evenly. Dip the glass rims in a little lightly beaten egg white, then into the coloured sugar.

Lime soda

METRIC/IMPERIAL/AMERICAN
1 small banana
3 tablespoons/3 tablespoons/$\frac{1}{4}$ cup lime cordial
1 family brick vanilla ice cream
250 ml/scant $\frac{1}{2}$ pint/1 cup soda water
slices of lime or lemon to decorate

Place the banana, lime cordial and half of the ice cream in the liquidiser. Switch on to a medium speed and blend until smooth and frothy.

Pour into glasses and float the remaining ice cream on top. Top each glass up with soda water and serve with a lime or lemon slice on the rim of each glass.

Serves 4

Tipsy orange flip

METRIC/IMPERIAL/AMERICAN
juice of 2 oranges
2 teaspoons lemon juice
2 eggs, separated
2 tablespoons/2 tablespoons/3 tablespoons sherry
25 g/1 oz/2 tablespoons sugar
2 cinnamon sticks

Place the orange and lemon juices in the liquidiser with the egg yolks, sherry and sugar. Switch on to a high speed and blend until well mixed.

Place the egg whites in the mixer bowl and whisk until fairly stiff. Fold into the blended mixture and serve immediately with a cinnamon stick in each glass.

Serves 2

Yogurt fruit shake

METRIC/IMPERIAL/AMERICAN
150 ml/¼ pint/⅔ cup fruit yogurt
½ banana
1 teaspoon honey
1 ice cube
2 tablespoons/2 tablespoons/3 tablespoons vanilla ice cream to decorate

Place all the ingredients in the liquidiser and blend until frothy. Pour into a glass and serve immediately with the ice cream floating on top.

Serves 1

Raspberry cooler

METRIC/IMPERIAL/AMERICAN
300 ml/½ pint/1¼ cups milk
150 ml/¼ pint/⅔ cup raspberry yogurt
100 g/4 oz/1 cup raspberries

Place the milk, raspberry yogurt and most of the raspberries, reserving some for decoration, in the liquidiser. Blend until mixture becomes frothy. Pour into glasses and float the reserved raspberries on top.

Serves 2

Brandy flip with clotted cream

METRIC/IMPERIAL/AMERICAN
2 eggs, separated
150 ml/¼ pint/⅔ cup brandy
2 tablespoons/2 tablespoons/3 tablespoons rum
150 ml/¼ pint/⅔ cup milk
sugar to taste
150 ml/¼ pint/⅔ cup clotted cream
nutmeg to decorate

Place the egg yolks in the liquidiser and mix for 2–3 seconds. Pour in the brandy, rum and milk. Blend until combined and pour into a bowl. Add sugar to taste. Chill.

Place the egg whites in the mixer bowl and whisk until fairly stiff. Fold into the brandy mixture. Pour into glasses. Top with clotted cream and sprinkle with nutmeg.

Serves 2

Minted chocolate

METRIC/IMPERIAL/AMERICAN
600 ml/1 pint/2½ cups milk
few drops of peppermint essence
1 family block vanilla ice cream
green food colouring
grated chocolate to decorate

Pour the milk into the liquidiser with the peppermint essence
and mix for 3–4 seconds. Cut the ice cream into cubes and add
to the liquidiser with a few drops of green colouring. Blend
until well mixed and smooth. Pour into glasses and decorate
with grated chocolate.

Serves 2–4

Hot mocha creams

METRIC/IMPERIAL/AMERICAN
600 ml/1 pint/2½ cups milk
1 tablespoon instant coffee
1 tablespoon cocoa powder
sugar to taste
2 tablespoons/2 tablespoons/3 tablespoons whipped
    cream

Heat the milk gently and stir in the coffee and cocoa. Pour into
the liquidiser and blend until frothy. Add the sugar to taste.
Pour into large mugs and top with a spoonful of whipped
cream.

Serves 3–4

Orange frappé

METRIC/IMPERIAL/AMERICAN
1 (178-ml/6¼-fl oz/6¼-fl oz) can concentrated frozen
    orange juice
24 ice cubes, lightly crushed
4 tablespoons/4 tablespoons/⅓ cup gin or vodka

Place all the ingredients in the liquidiser and blend until the mixture resembles crushed ice. Spoon into frosted glasses and serve immediately.

Variation: Substitute concentrated grapefruit juice for the orange juice.
To frost glasses, dip the rims of glasses in a little beaten egg white and then in castor sugar. Allow to harden before spooning in the frappé.

Serves 4

Honeyed lemonade

METRIC/IMPERIAL/AMERICAN
2 thin-skinned lemons
50 g/2 oz/¼ cup sugar
2 tablespoons/2 tablespoons/3 tablespoons clear honey
600 ml/1 pint/2½ cups water
slices of lemon to decorate

Roughly chop the lemons and place in the liquidiser with the sugar, honey and water. Blend until mixed, then strain into a jug. Serve chilled with a lemon slice on the rim of each glass.

Serves 2